P9-CMS-721

Janice VanCleave's

203

Icy,
Freezing,
Frosty,
Cool & Wild
Experiments

John Wiley & Sons, Inc.

New York · Chichester · Weinheim · Brisbane · Singapore · Toronto

This book is printed on acid-free paper. ∞

Copyright © 1999 by Janice VanCleave. All rights reserved
Published by John Wiley & Sons, Inc.
Published simultaneously in Canada

Portions of this book have been reprinted from the books *Janice VanCleave's Astronomy for Every Kid, Janice VanCleave's A+ Projects in Earth Science, Janice VanCleave's A+ Projects in Chemistry, Janice VanCleave's Guide to the Best Science Fair Projects, Janice VanCleave's Constellations for Every Kid, Janice VanCleave's Dinosaurs for Every Kid, Janice VanCleave's Ecology for Every Kid, Janice VanCleave's Electricity, Janice VanCleave's Geography for Every Kid, Janice VanCleave's Gravity, Janice VanCleave's The Human Body for Every Kid, Janice VanCleave's Insects and Spiders, Janice VanCleave's Machines, Janice VanCleave's Molecules, Janice VanCleave's Oceans for Every Kid, Janice VanCleave's Plants, Janice VanCleave's Play and Find Out about Bugs, Janice VanCleave's Play and Find Out about Science, Janice VanCleave's Rocks and Minerals, Janice VanCleave's Volcanoes,* and *Janice VanCleave's Weather.*

No part of this publication may be reproduced, stored in a retrieval system, or transmitted in any form or by any means, electronic, mechanical, photocopying, recording, scanning, or otherwise, except as permitted under Section 107 or 108 of the 1976 United States Copyright Act, without either the prior written permission of the Publisher, or authorization through payment of the appropriate per-copy fee to the Copyright Clearance Center, 222 Rosewood Drive, Danvers, MA 01923, (978) 750-8400, fax (978) 750-4744. Requests to the Publisher for permission should be addressed to the Permissions Department, John Wiley & Sons, Inc., 605 Third Avenue, New York, NY 10158-0012, (212) 850-6011, fax (212) 850-6008, e-mail PERMREQ@WILEY.COM.

The Publisher and the author have made every reasonable effort to ensure that the experiments and activities in this book are safe when conducted as instructed but assume no responsibility for any damage caused or sustained while performing the experiments or activities in the book. Parents, guardians, and/or teachers should supervise young readers who undertake the experiments and activities in this book.

Library of Congress Cataloging-in-Publication Data

VanCleave, Janice Pratt
    Janice VanCleave's 203 icy, freezing, frosty, cool & wild experiments
      p.   cm.
    Includes index.
    ISBN 0-471-25223-9 (pbk.)
    1. Science—Experiments—Study and teaching. 2. Science—Experiments—
Juvenile literature. I. Title. II. Title: Janice VanCleave's two hundred and three icy,
freezing, frosty, cool and wild experiments. III. Title: 203 icy, freezing, frosty, cool &
wild experiments.
    Q182.3.V35   1999
    507.8—dc21
                                                             98-49721
                                                                CIP

Printed in the United States of America

10 9 8 7 6 5 4 3 2

Dedication

It is a pleasure to dedicate this book to E. Robert Fanick and Virginia Malone.

Robert Fanick is a chemist at Southwest Research Institute in San Antonio, Texas, and Virginia Malone is a science assessment consultant. These two very special people have provided a great deal of valuable information, which has made this book even more understandable and fun.

Acknowledgments

I wish to express my appreciation to these science specialists for their valuable assistance by providing information or assisting me in finding it.

Members of the Central Texas Astronomical Society, including Johnny Barton, John W. McAnally, and Paul Derrick: Johnny is an officer of the club and has been an active amateur astronomer for more than 20 years. John is also on the staff of The Association of Lunar and Planetary Observers where he is acting Assistant Coordinator for Transit Timings of the Jupiter Section. Paul is the author of the "Stargazer" column in the Waco *Tribune-Herald*.

Dr. Glenn S. Orton, a Senior Research Scientist at the Jet Propulsion Laboratory of California Institute of Technology: Glenn is an astronomer and space scientist who specializes in investigating the structure and composition of planetary atmospheres. He is best known for his research on Jupiter and Saturn. I have enjoyed exchanging ideas with Glenn about experiments for modeling astronomy experiments.

A special note of gratitude to these educators who assisted by pretesting the activities and/or by providing scientific information: Holly Harris, China Spring Intermediate, China Spring, Texas; Laura Roberts, St. Matthews Elementary, Louisville, Kentucky; James Roberts, Oldham County High School, Buckner, Kentucky.

I would also like to extend a special thanks to Randy Landsberg, the Director of Education & Outreach from The Center for Astrophysical Research in Antarctica (CARA) at the University of Chicago. Randy invited me to accompany him to the South Pole. Sponsored by the National Science Foundation, the objective of our trip was to encourage student interest in science and Antarctica. The scientific research of CARA is supported through Cooperative Agreement No. 89-20223 from the National Science Foundation to the University of Chicago. Information from the trip and research as a result of the trip served as the foundation for some of the experiments in this book.

Contents

Introduction

This book is a collection of science experiments designed to show you that science is more than a list of facts—science is fun! The 203 experiments in the book take science out of the laboratory and put it into your daily life.

Science is a way of solving problems and discovering why things happen the way they do. Why does the Moon have different shapes? How can whales use sound to "see"? How do rocks form? You'll find the answers to these and many other questions by doing the experiments in this book.

The experiments cover five different fields of science:

- **Astronomy**   The study of the planets, the stars, and other bodies in space.
- **Biology**   The study of the way living organisms behave and interact.
- **Chemistry**   The study of the way materials are put together and their behavior under different conditions.
- **Earth Science**   The study of Earth.
- **Physics**   The study of energy and matter and their relationships.

The Experiments

Scientists identify a problem, or an event, and seek solutions, or explanations, through research and documentation. A goal of this book is to guide you through the steps necessary to successfully complete a science experiment and to teach you the best method of solving problems and discovering answers.

1. **Purpose:**   The basic goals for the experiment.
2. **Materials:**   A list of necessary supplies.
3. **Procedure:**   Step-by-step instructions on how to perform the experiment.
4. **Results:**   An explanation stating exactly what is expected to happen. This is an immediate learning tool. If the expected results are achieved, the experimenter has an immediate positive reinforcement. An error is also quickly recognized, and the need to start over or make corrections is readily apparent.
5. **Why?**   An explanation of why the results were achieved is descried in terms that are understandable to the reader, who may not be familiar with scientific terms. When a new term is introduced and explained, it appears in **bold** type; these terms can also be found in the Glossary.

You will be rewarded with successful experiments if you read each experiment carefully, follow the steps in order, and do not substitute materials.

General Instructions

1. **Read first.** Read each experiment completely before starting.
2. **Collect needed supplies.** You will experience less frustration and more fun if you gather all the necessary materials for the experiments before you begin. You lose your train of thought when you have to stop and search for supplies.
3. **Experiment.** Follow each step very carefully, never skip steps, and do not add your own. Safety is of the utmost importance, and by reading the experiment before starting, then following the instructions exactly, you can feel confident that no unexpected results will occur.
4. **Observe.** If your results are not the same as described in the experiment, carefully read the instructions and start over from the first step.

Measurements

Measuring quantities described in this book are intended to be those commonly used in every kitchen. When specific amounts are given, you need to use a measuring instrument closest to the described amount. The quantities listed are not critical, and a variation of very small amounts more or less will not alter the results. Approximate metric equivalents are given in parentheses.

1. Blinding

Purpose To demonstrate how the Sun's light affects the visibility of Venus.

Materials   scissors   white chalk
drawing compass   transparent tape
ruler   pencil
black construction paper   flashlight

Procedure

1. Cut a circle with a diameter of about 2 inches (5 cm) from the black paper.
2. Use the chalk to mark an X about ¼ inch (0.63 cm) high anywhere near the edge of the paper circle.
3. Tape the blank back of the paper to the end of the pencil. This will be your model of Venus.
4. Lay the flashlight on a table and turn it on. The flashlight represents the Sun. Darken the room.
5. Grasp the end of the pencil and hold it so that the side of the paper with the chalk mark faces you.
6. Hold the pencil at arm's length from your face and about 6 inches (15 cm) in front of the flashlight. Observe the surface of the paper.
7. Move the paper above the light about 4 inches (10 cm) and again observe the surface of the paper.
8. Repeat step 7, moving the paper below the light.

Results When the paper is held in front of the light, the white mark is difficult or impossible to see. When the paper is held above and below the light, the white mark may become more visible, but not much.

Why? The light behind the paper is so bright that it is difficult to see the surface of the paper. In a similar way, the glare of the Sun behind the planet Venus makes it difficult to see Venus. Objects in the sky, such as stars, suns, moons, and planets, are **celestial bodies. Celestial** means heavenly. Venus is the second planet from the Sun, Earth being the third. In its **orbit** (the path of one body around another) around the Sun, as viewed from Earth, Venus is never far from the Sun in the sky because it is so close to the Sun in relation to Earth. Even when Venus is at its farthest point from the Sun, it is difficult to see the planet when the Sun and the planet are both above the **horizon** (an imaginary line where the sky appears to meet Earth). The best time to see Venus, therefore, is before the Sun comes up or after the Sun goes down.

2. Long and Short

Purpose To model the relationship between shadow length and the movement of the Sun.

Materials   scissors
ruler
drinking straw
grape-size piece of modeling clay
flashlight

Procedure

1. Cut one 2-inch (5-cm) piece from the straw.
2. Use the clay to stand the piece of straw on a table. The straw should be **perpendicular** (at a right angle) to the table.
3. In a darkened room, hold the flashlight on the left side of the straw about 6 inches (15 cm) away. The light should be pointed toward the top of the straw.
4. Slowly move the flashlight directly over the straw, then to the right, in an **arc** (part of a circle) as shown in the figure. Observe the length of the straw's shadow as the flashlight moves from position 1 to position 3.

Results The shadow of the straw is long when the flashlight is pointing from either side. It shortens as the light moves to an overhead position.

Why? Earth **rotates,** which means it turns on its **axis** (an imaginary line that passes through the center of an object and around which the object rotates). As Earth rotates, the Sun appears to rise in the morning and travel in an arc across the sky. In the morning, when the Sun is low in the sky, the shadows of objects are long. At noon, the Sun is at its highest **altitude** (angular distance above the horizon) in the sky and shadows are shortest. In the afternoon, shadow lengths increase as the Sun's altitude decreases.

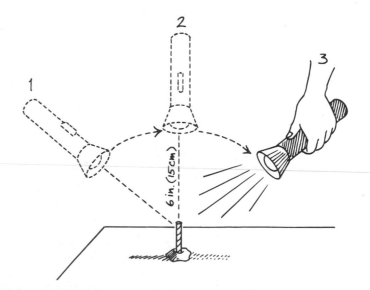

I
Astronomy

3. Circular Path

Purpose To model the movement of the Sun's path at Earth's poles.

Materials 5 tablespoons (75 ml) plaster of paris
2 tablespoons (30 ml) tap water
3-ounce (90-ml) paper cup
pencil
white poster board
20-inch (50-cm) piece of string
flashlight
transparent tape

Procedure

CAUTION: Do not wash plaster down the drain. It can clog the drain.

1. Mix the plaster of paris and water together in the cup with the writing end of the pencil.
2. Stand the pencil vertically in the plaster. Allow the plaster to dry. This may take 30 minutes or more.
3. Lay the poster board on a table and set the cup of dry plaster in the center of the poster board.
4. Tie one end of the string to the bulb end of the flashlight and tape the other end to the top of the craft stick.
5. In a darkened room, hold the flashlight so that the string is straight and the flashlight is level with the top of the stick.
6. Move the flashlight in a circle around the stick, keeping the string straight and the flashlight level with the top of the stick.

7. Observe the direction and length of the stick's shadow as you move the flashlight.

Results The shadow length remains about the same as it moves in a circular path around the stick.

Why? The **equator** is an imaginary line that circles Earth midway between the **North** and **South Poles** (northernmost and southernmost points on Earth). When it is summer in the **Northern Hemisphere** (the region of Earth north of the equator), the Sun never sets at the North Pole. Instead, it remains at about the same position relative to the horizon, as it appears to move across the sky. At the same time, it never rises at the South Pole. The same thing happens when it is summer in the **Southern Hemisphere** (the region of Earth south of the equator). At the poles, the Sun's greatest altitude is 23.5° above the horizon. (Keep the cup of plaster for Experiment 7, "Angled.")

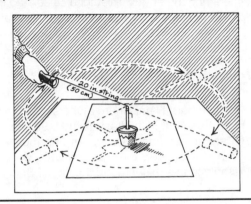

4. Overhead

Purpose To model the highest altitude of the Sun.

Materials 6-inch (15-cm) piece of string
protractor with a hole in the center of its base
ruler
two 1-inch (2.6-cm) round orange labels
pen

Procedure

1. Thread one end of the string through the hole in the protractor and tie a knot.
2. About 4 inches (10 cm) from the protractor's base, place the sticky sides of the labels together on the string so that the string is sandwiched between them. Write Sun on the labels and draw sunrays.
3. Set the straight edge of the protractor on a table. Holding the protractor in place with one hand, extend the string up to the 90° mark on the protractor with your other hand. Observe the position of the labels.

NOTE: Keep the model to use in the next experiment.

Results A model is made showing the altitude of the Sun when it is directly overhead.

Why? Directly overhead means that the Sun is at an altitude of 90°. The Sun is only ever directly overhead at or between **latitudes** (distances measured in degrees north and south of the equator) 23.5°N and 23.5°S. At **summer solstice,** the longest day of the year, the Sun is directly

overhead at latitude 23.5°N, in the Northern Hemisphere (on or about June 21), and at latitude 23.5°S, in the Southern Hemisphere (on or about December 22). During summer solstice in one hemisphere, it is **winter solstice,** the shortest day of the year, in the opposite hemisphere, and the Sun is at its lowest altitude. At **vernal** (spring) and **autumnal equinoxes,** on or about March 21 and September 23 respectively, the Sun is directly overhead at the equator, latitude 0°. The days are of equal length at the equator all year, but at the equinoxes the days and nights are of equal length all around Earth.

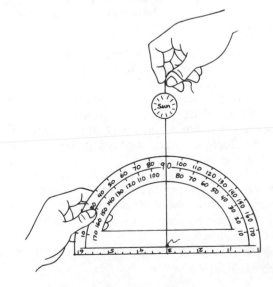

5. Lower

Purpose To determine the highest altitude the Sun reaches at your town's latitude.

Materials model from Experiment 4, "Overhead"

Procedure
1. Find your town's latitude by looking at a map or asking an adult, such as your teacher, librarian, or parent.
2. Determine the angular difference between your town's latitude and latitude 23.5°. For example, at Buffalo, New York, at latitude 43°N, the difference would be 43° − 23.5° = 19.5°
3. Lay the model on a table with the straight edge facing you. Stretch the string across the 90° mark on the protractor.
4. Move the string the angular distance calculated in step 2 below the 90° mark. In the example for Buffalo, the string is moved 19.5° below 90°. Where does the string cross the protractor?

Results In the example, the string crosses the 70.5° mark on the protractor.

Why? In the Northern Hemisphere at the summer solstice (June 21), the Sun is at its highest altitude, 90° above the **Tropic of Cancer** (latitude 23.5°N). As one moves away from the Tropic of Cancer, the Sun's altitude decreases. For the example in this experiment, the city of Buffalo was

calculated to be 19.5° north of the latitude 23.5°N. This means that on June 21, the Sun is 19.5° lower in the sky in Buffalo than in a city at latitude 23.5°N. On June 21 at the Tropic of Cancer, the Sun is directly overhead, or at an altitude of 90°. On the same date, the Sun's altitude decreases as one moves north. In Buffalo, the Sun is 19.5° lower than 90°, or at an altitude of 70.5° above the horizon. In the Southern Hemisphere at the summer solstice (December 22), the Sun is at its highest altitude of 90° above the **Tropic of Capricorn** (latitude 23.5°S). As in the Northern Hemisphere, the Sun's altitude decreases as one moves away from the Tropic of Capricorn.

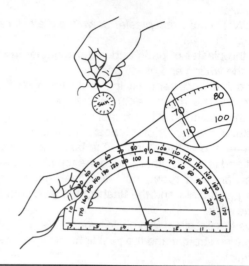

6. Sun Time

Purpose To determine the difference between your local sun time and clock time.

Materials pen
ruler
4 × 8-inch (10 × 20-cm) piece of corrugated cardboard
watch
directional compass
grape-size ball of clay
short pencil, about 2 inches (5 cm) long

Procedure
1. Use the pen and ruler to draw a 6-inch (15-cm) line down the center of the cardboard. Mark one end of the line N and the other end S.
2. About 40 minutes before 12:00 P.M. (noon) on a sunny day, place the cardboard outdoors on a flat surface. Use the compass to point the N on the line north. *NOTE: Subtract 1 hour from your watch time if daylight saving time is in effect.*
3. Use the ball of clay to stand the pencil at the S end of the line. The pencil must be perpendicular to the line.
4. Observe the shadow of the pencil as it approaches the line. When the shadow is directly over the line, note the time on your watch.
5. Calculate the difference between the time on your watch and 12:00.

Results The difference between the times will vary depending on where you live.

Why? Imaginary lines circling the Earth from North Pole to South Pole are called **meridians.** These lines are measured in **longitude,** which is the distance in degrees east and west of the **prime meridian** running through Greenwich, England, at 0° longitude. In the experiment, the line on the paper represents your local meridian (longitude line). Earth is divided into 24 internationally agreed time zones. Each **time zone** is about 15° of longitude wide, and local time (clock time) is the same throughout any given time zone. Each zone is centered on a meridian called the time meridian, with about 7.5° of longitude on either side of the meridian. The local time within each time zone is called **standard time,** but the Sun time within each time zone is not the same throughout the zone at any given moment. This is because as Earth rotates, the Sun appears to move from east to west across the time zone. At noon (12 o'clock) local time at locations west of the time meridian, the Sun's sky position is generally more to the east, and at locations east of the time meridian, the Sun's sky position is generally more to the west.

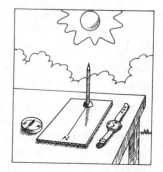

7. Angled

Purpose To make an instrument to measure the altitude of a light source such as the Sun.

Materials yardstick (meterstick)
protractor
masking tape
pencil
3 feet (1 m) of string
cup of plaster from Experiment 3, "Circular Path"
flashlight
ruler
writing paper
helper

Procedure

1. Place the measuring stick on a table. Stand the protractor alongside the measuring stick so the line between the 0° marks lines up with the edge of the stick. Tape the protractor to the stick. The end of the stick opposite the protractor will be called the pointer end.

2. Place a piece of tape across the measuring stick next to the center mark on the protractor. Make a mark across the tape from the center of the protractor. This mark will be called the measuring line.

3. Tear away the paper cup above the hardened plaster and tape one end of the string to the top of the pencil. Set the cup in the middle of the measuring stick.

4. Turn on the flashlight, then darken the room. Hold the cup in place with one hand and hold the flashlight in the other hand over the pointer end about 12 inches (30 cm) from the top of the pencil as shown. Move the cup until the tip of the pencil's shadow touches the measuring line.

5. Ask a helper to extend the string from the top of the pencil to the measuring line, then read the angle where the string crosses the protractor and record it as the altitude of the light.

6. Repeat steps 4 and 5 twice, first raising the flashlight higher, then lowering it. With each experiment, keep the distance between the flashlight and the pencil the same.

NOTE: Keep the instrument for the next experiment.

Results An instrument for measuring the altitude of a light source is made. The angle gets larger or smaller as the height of the light above the measuring stick increases or decreases, respectively.

Why? The greater the angle, the greater the altitude of the light. The instrument can be used for measuring the altitude of the Sun above the horizon. See the next experiment for instructions.

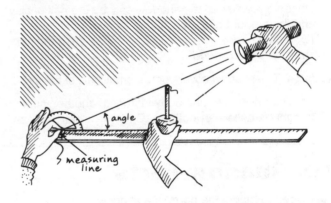

8. How High?

Purpose To measure the altitude of the Sun.

Materials instrument from Experiment 7, "Angled"
pen or pencil
writing paper
watch
helper

Procedure

CAUTION: Never look directly at the Sun. It can damage your eyes.

1. Take your instrument outdoors on a sunny day just before 11:00 A.M.

2. Set the measuring stick on a flat surface with its pointer end facing the horizon directly below the Sun.

3. Set the cup in the middle of the stick. Adjust the pointer end of the stick so that the shadow cast by the pencil falls on the stick.

4. Move the cup back and forth on the stick until the end of the shadow touches the measuring line.

5. Hold the cup in place and extend the string from the top of the pencil to the measuring line. Ask a helper to read the angle where the string crosses the protractor.

6. Repeat steps 2 through 5 every 15 minutes until 1:00 P.M. Compare the sizes of the angles.

NOTE: If the shadow is longer than the measuring stick, place two measuring sticks end to end.

Results The angle size increases and then decreases at the same rate.

Why? The angle measured is equal to the altitude of the Sun. In the early morning, the Sun is at a low altitude, so the angle is small. As the Sun gets higher in the sky, approaching its highest altitude at or near what is called **solar** noon, the angle increases. After solar noon as the Sun gets lower in the sky, the angle decreases.

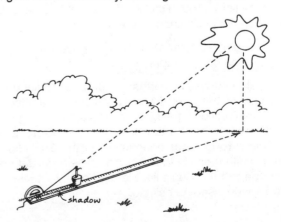

9. Blackout

Purpose To demonstrate why the whole Earth is not darkened by a solar eclipse.

Materials   drawing compass
ruler
sheet of white poster board
black marker
lemon-size ball of clay
pencil

Procedure

1. Use the compass to draw a 20-inch (50-cm) diameter circle in the center of the poster board.
2. Use the marker to label the circle Earth.
3. Place the poster board on the ground in a sunny area outside.
4. Stick the clay ball on the eraser end of the pencil. Push the point of the pencil through the center of the circle and into the ground so that the pencil stands upright.
5. Observe the size of the shadow cast by the ball of clay and the amount of the circle that it covers.

NOTE: If the shadow falls outside the circle, push the pencil farther into the ground.

Results The shadow covers only a small part of the circle.

Why? The passing of one body in front of another, cutting off its light, is called an **eclipse**. During a **solar eclipse**, the Moon comes between the Sun and Earth so that the Moon's shadow falls on the surface of Earth. The Moon's shadow, like the shadow of the clay ball, only covers a small area. Thus, most of Earth is not darkened during a solar eclipse. For more information about the Moon's shadow, see the next experiment.

10. Shadow Parts

Purpose To model the parts of a shadow.

Materials   ruler
sharpened pencil
3-inch (7.5-cm) Styrofoam ball
sheet of typing paper
flashlight

Procedure

1. Insert about ½ inch (1.25 cm) of the pointed end of the pencil into the Styrofoam ball.
2. Lay the paper on a table.
3. In a darkened room, hold the ball about 4 inches (10 cm) above the paper.
4. Hold the light about 8 inches (20 cm) above the ball.
5. Observe the ball's shadow on the paper.

Results A dark circular shadow surrounded by a lighter circle is formed on the paper.

Why? A shadow has two parts: the **umbra** (darker part of a shadow) and the **penumbra** (lighter part of a shadow). During a solar eclipse, the Moon blocks the Sun's light and casts a shadow on Earth. Observers on Earth in the umbra see a **total solar eclipse** (all of the Sun's light is blocked), while those in the penumbra see a **partial solar eclipse** (part of the Sun's light is blocked) and those outside the shadow see no eclipse.

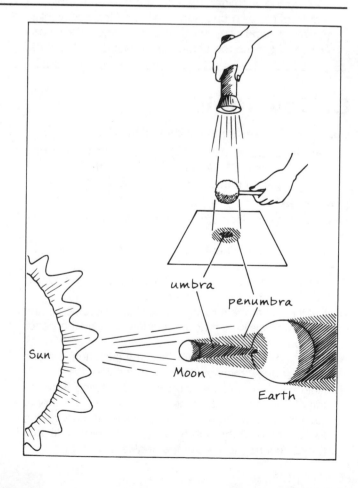

11. Finding North

Purpose To find compass directions during the daytime.

Materials your shadow

Procedure
1. Stand outdoors on a sunny day at solar noon (when the sun is at its highest altitude and casts the shortest shadows).
2. Face your shadow. You are facing north, and directly behind you is south.
3. Hold your arms out to your sides. Your right hand points to the east, your left to the west.

Results A Sun's shadow is used to find general compass directions.

Why? In the Northern Hemisphere, shadows point north at solar noon (south, if you are in the Southern Hemisphere). Using shadows at solar noon, one can find the other compass directions. East is to your right, West to your left, and South behind you.

12. Moon Size

Purpose To show how the Moon's distance from Earth affects its apparent size.

Materials grape-size ball of clay
2 sharpened pencils
3-inch (7.5-cm) Styrofoam ball

Procedure
1. Place the ball of clay on the point of one of the pencils and the Styrofoam ball on the other pencil's point.
2. Hold the pencil with the Styrofoam ball at arm's length so that the ball is in front of your face.
3. Close one eye and hold the pencil with the clay ball so that the ball is in front of but not touching your open eye. Slowly move the clay ball away from your face toward the Styrofoam ball. As you move the clay ball, observe how much of the Styrofoam ball is hidden by the clay ball at different distances.

Results The closer the clay ball is to your face, the more it hides the Styrofoam ball.

Why? The closer an object is to your eye, the bigger it appears. The small ball of clay can totally block your view of the larger Styrofoam ball. In the same way, the Moon, which has a diameter of 2,173 miles (3,476 km), can block your view of the much larger Sun, which has a diameter of 870,000 miles (1.39 million km).

During a solar eclipse, when the Moon passes directly between the Sun and Earth, the Moon, the Sun, and Earth are in a straight line. In this position, the Moon blocks the view of the Sun from a viewer on Earth. Even though the Moon is about 400 times smaller than the Sun, it is about 400 times nearer Earth than is the Sun. This makes their size look about the same from Earth.

13. Moon Watch

Purpose To observe the Moon's phases.

Materials sheet of typing paper
pen
ruler
newspaper or calendar with moon phases

Procedure

1. Use the paper, pen, and ruler to draw a calendar for 5 weeks.
2. Fill in the dates on the calendar, starting with the day you prepare the calendar. Note that the calendar may include parts of 2 months.
3. Observe the shape of the Moon for 29 days. Draw the shape of the Moon for each day on the data calendar. For day 1 of observation, check the newspaper or calendar with moon phases listed, then check the Times of Moonrise and Moonset table for observation times for the moon phase for that day.

NOTE: Make no observation for at least 3 days before and after new moon—when the side of the moon facing Earth is dark. The new moon is close to the Sun and you could damage your eyes if you look at it.

TIMES OF MOONRISE AND MOONSET

Phase	Moonrise	Moonset
New	dawn	sunset
First Quarter	noon	midnight
Full	sunset	dawn
Third Quarter	midnight	noon

Results It takes about 29 days for the Moon to return to the same shape observed on the first night of observation.

Why? The apparent changes in the Moon's shape are called **moon phases.** Phases are seen because the Moon **revolves** (moves around a center point) around Earth. As it revolves, different amounts of the side of the Moon facing Earth are lighted by the Sun. The **waxing** (growing larger) phases as shown are **new, crescent, first quarter, gibbous,** and **full.** Following the full moon, the moon goes through the same phases in reverse. These phases are said to be **waning,** and the quarter phase is call the **third quarter.** The diagram shows the visible lighted surface in each of the Moon's phases.

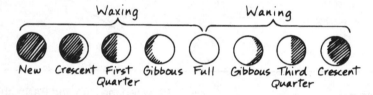

14. Earthshine

Purpose To demonstrate why the faint outline of the entire Moon is visible during the crescent moon phase.

Materials lemon-size piece of blue modeling clay
craft stick
flashlight
3 to 4 books
ruler
cotton ball

Procedure

1. Divide the clay in half and roll it into two balls.
2. Stick a ball on each end of the craft stick.
3. Press one clay piece onto a table to stand the other ball upright. This upper ball will be your Moon model.
4. Next to the model, stack the books and lay the flashlight on top so that its bulb is about 2 inches (5 cm) from the clay moon. Turn on the flashlight.
5. In a darkened room, observe the dark side of the clay. Hold the cotton ball about 4 inches (10 cm) away from and to one side of the clay moon, and again observe the dark side of the clay.

Results When you first observed the dark side of the clay moon, it was hard to see any of the surface. When you held the cotton ball near the dark side, the surface of the clay became a bit lighter.

Why? Light reflects off the cotton ball and illuminates the dark surface of the clay. (The blue color of clay is not significant; any dark-colored surface will be illuminated.) In the same way, sunlight is reflected from Earth's surface onto the Moon. This reflected light is called **earthshine.** Earthshine is happening all the time, but the effect of this reflected light on the Moon is more visible during the crescent moon phase. The faint outline of the entire Moon is visible during this phase. This phenomenon is sometimes referred to as the "old moon in the new moon's arms."

15. The Light Side

Purpose To demonstrate why only one side of the Moon is visible from Earth.

Materials   drawing compass
sheet of typing paper
pencil
marble-size ball of clay
small paper clip

Procedure

1. Use the compass to draw a large circle on the paper to represent the orbit of the Moon. Make a small circle in the center of the large circle to represent Earth.
2. Make a mark on the edge of the Moon circle. This will be the starting point of the Moon's revolution around Earth.
3. Stick the point of the pencil into the ball of clay, then insert the paper clip in the center of one side of the clay. Stand the pencil next to the starting mark so that the paper clip faces the Earth circle.
4. Slowly move the pencil counterclockwise once along the Moon circle, rotating the pencil just enough to keep the paper clip facing the center of the Earth circle. Observe the rotation of the paper clip to determine how many times the clay ball rotates as you move it along the Moon circle.

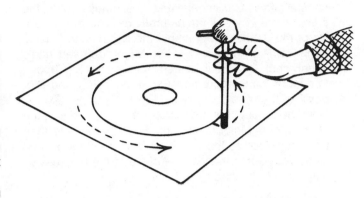

Results The paper clip rotates once, showing that the clay ball makes one rotation on its axis as it moves once along the Moon circle.

Why? The Moon makes one complete rotation as it revolves once around Earth. This motion is called **synchronous rotation.** Because of synchronous rotation, the same side of the Moon is always visible from Earth.

16. Moonlight

Purpose To distinguish between luminous and nonluminous celestial bodies.

Materials   4-inch (10-cm) -square piece of aluminum foil
transparent tape
4-inch (10-cm) piece of string
large shoe box with lid
ruler
scissors
flashlight

Procedure

1. Crumple the aluminum foil into a grape-size ball and tape one end of the string to the aluminum ball.
2. Turn the shoe-box lid upside down, and tape the free end of the string about 2 inches (5 cm) from the corner as shown.
3. Cut a ½-by-2-inch (1.25-by-5-cm) flap about 2 inches (5 cm) from the right corner of one short side of the box. Cut a 1-by-2-inch (2.5-by-5-cm) flap about 1 inch from the opposite corner of the same side.
4. Close the large flap and place the lid on the box so that the ball hangs at the opposite end from the small, open flap.
5. Set the box on a table and look through the open flap toward the ball. Make note of the visibility of the hanging ball.
6. Raise the lid and open the large flap.
7. Repeat steps 5 and 6, shining the flashlight through the open flap toward the hanging ball inside the box.

Results The aluminum ball is not visible or only slightly visible without the light from the flashlight. With the light from the flashlight, the ball appears shiny.

Why? In this experiment, the ball represents the Moon, and the flashlight, the Sun. The Moon, like the model, is not **luminous** (giving off its own light). The Moon shines mainly because light from the Sun, a luminous body, reflects off it. A small amount of the Moon's brightness is due to a double reflection. First, sunlight reflects off Earth to the Moon, where it is reflected back to Earth. This brightness of the Moon is called earthshine.

17. Sky Ball

Purpose To make a model of the celestial sphere.

Materials   gummed stars
umbrella with 8 sections (preferably a solid, dark color)

Procedure

1. Using the gummed stars to represent the stars of the constellations Cassiopeia and Ursa Major, stick the stars on the inside of the umbrella as shown. The center of the umbrella represents the North Star, Polaris. (Only some of the stars in Ursa Major are used in this experiment. This group of stars is called the Big Dipper. For more information, see Experiment 20, "The Dipper.")
2. Hold the umbrella at a slant above your head with the stars of Ursa Major to your left. Face these stars, then turn your head to the right and face the stars of Cassiopeia. Observe the inside surface of the umbrella as you move your head.

Results When you start, you see only the constellation Ursa Major. As you turn your head, Cassiopeia comes into view.

Why? A **constellation** such as Ursa Major or Cassiopeia is a group of stars that appear to make a pattern in the sky. Astronomers have designed an imaginary sphere called the **celestial sphere** to help locate constellations and other celestial bodies. Earth is pictured at the center of this large, hollow sphere with all other celestial bodies stuck on its inside surface. The umbrella in this experiment is a model of the celestial sphere. Turning your head represents Earth's west-to-east rotation. From any given location on Earth, a different part of the sky is seen as Earth rotates. In the Northern Hemisphere, Earth's axis, represented by the umbrella's center shaft, points toward **Polaris,** or the **North Star.** The location in the sky where Earth's axis points is called a **celestial pole.** Polaris is near the north celestial pole. Thus, it is also called the **Pole Star.**

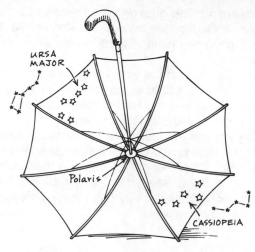

18. Movers

Purpose To observe the apparent movement of stars.

Materials   poster board
marker
2 bricks, rocks, or other heavy objects
watch
helper

Procedure

1. On a clear moonless night, go outside and find a group of stars that are near the edge of a landmark, such as the roof of your house, a tree, or a telephone pole.
2. Place the poster board on the ground and stand on it. Again locate the same group of stars near the edge of the landmark. Move the poster board if necessary.
3. Ask your helper to use the marker to trace around your feet on the poster board, then to secure the poster board to the ground with the bricks, rocks, or other heavy objects.
4. While standing on the poster board, make a mental note of how close the stars appear to the edge of the landmark.
5. Step off the poster board without moving it.
6. Repeat steps 4 and 5 every hour for 3 hours or more.

Results The star group moves in relation to your landmark.

Why? As Earth rotates from west to east, the stars appear to move across the sky. The diagram shows the direction of motion of the star group depending on whether you are facing north, south, east, or west.

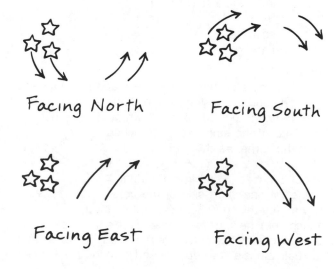

19. Shifting

Purpose To demonstrate parallax movement.

Materials 3-foot (1-m) strip of adding-machine paper
marking pen
masking tape
pencil

Procedure

1. Fold the adding-machine paper in half four times.
2. Unfold the paper, draw an arrow on the center fold, and number the folds 1 through 7 on each side of the arrow as shown.
3. Tape the paper to a wall at about eye level.
4. Stand in front of the arrow, then walk backward six steps.
5. Hold the pencil upright in front of, but not touching, your nose. The top of the pencil should be about even with the top of your eyes.
6. Close your left eye and notice the mark on the paper that the pencil appears to be in line with or closest to.
7. Without moving your head or the pencil, open your left eye and close your right eye. Notice the mark on the paper that the pencil appears to be in line with or closest to.
8. Repeat steps 5 through 7, holding the pencil at arm's length.

Results The pencil first appears to move toward the left, then toward the right. This movement is less when the pencil is held at a distance from your face.

Why? One method that astronomers use to find the distance of nearby stars is to measure their **parallax** (the apparent shift in position of an object when viewed from different places). In this experiment, the pencil seems to jump from side to side as you look at it with each eye separately. Each of your eyes views the pencil from a different angle. Thus, the background of the pencil is different for each eye. Stars, like the pencil, seem to move when viewed from different points on Earth's orbit. The farther the star, the smaller the parallax.

20. The Dipper

Purpose To locate an asterism.

Materials directional compass

Procedure

1. During the day, use the compass to determine the direction of north.
2. Find a place that provides the best view of the northern part of the sky.
3. Go outside on a clear moonless night and stand in the designated spot facing north.
4. Look for seven stars that form the shape of a large dipper.

NOTE: *The bowl of the dipper faces different directions, even upside down, at different times.*

Results A group of stars called the Big Dipper is found.

Why? The Big Dipper is an **asterism** (a group of stars that form a shape within a constellation). Ursa Major (the Great Bear) is the constellation that Big Dipper is a part of. Once you find the Big Dipper, search for the rest of Ursa Major. It is easiest to find in the spring, when it is high above the northern horizon.

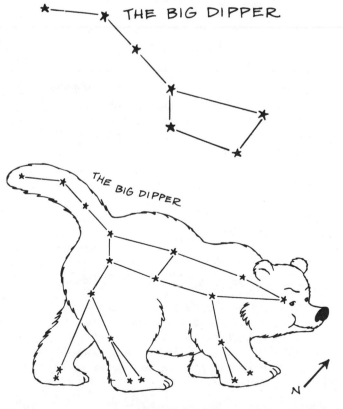

THE BIG DIPPER

THE BIG DIPPER

URSA MAJOR

21. North Star

Purpose To locate the star Polaris.

Materials your body

Procedure
1. Go outside on a clear, moonless night.
2. Find the Big Dipper (see the previous experiment). Mentally draw a line in the sky, passing through the two stars in the front of the dipper to Polaris, as shown in the diagram.

Results Polaris is located.

Why? The stars in the Big Dipper, Merak and Dubhe, are called the pointers. An imaginary line drawn through these stars, starting with Merak and continuing past Dubhe, points to Polaris.

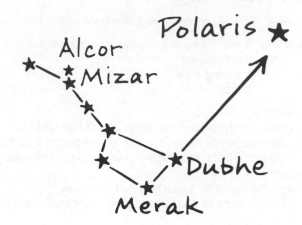

22. Sky Compass

Purpose To use Polaris to find directions in the Northern Hemisphere.

Materials your body

Purpose
1. Go outside on a clear moonless night and face north by finding Polaris. (Use the information from the previous experiment to find Polaris.)
2. Facing Polaris, hold your arms straight out to your sides.

Results In front of you is the direction north, behind you is south, to your right is east, and to your left is west.

Why? Once you find Polaris, you can use the star at any time to find direction in the Northern Hemisphere. It is called the Pole Star or North Star because it appears to remain in the same place in the sky—almost exactly above Earth's North Pole—night after night. When you are facing Polaris, east is to your right, west is to your left, and south is directly behind you.

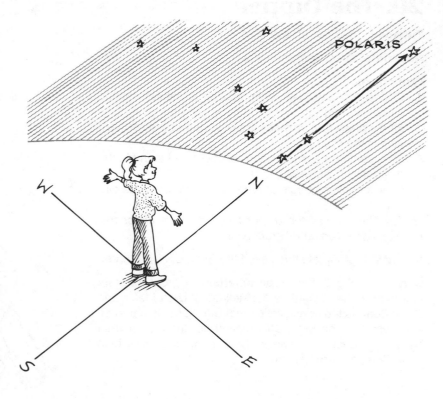

23. Above the Horizon

Purpose To determine how Polaris can appear to be in different positions above the horizon.

Materials masking tape   yardstick (meterstick)
3 feet (1 m) of string   marking pen
penny   index card
ruler   adult helper

Procedure

1. Tape one end of the string to the coin.
2. Ask your adult helper to tape the free end of the string to the center of the top of a doorjamb so that the coin hangs about 6 inches (15 cm) over your head when you stand in the doorway.
   NOTE: Choose a doorway leading into a second room that has a far wall.
3. Place a piece of masking tape about 1 inch (2.5 cm) long on the floor beneath the hanging coin. Mark an X on the tape.
4. Draw a thick straight line across the center of the index card. Write Horizon beneath the line.
5. Measure 6 feet (1.8 m) from the X to a point on the floor of the first room, and place another piece of tape on the floor. Mark this tape with an E.
6. Stand behind the tape labeled E, close one eye, and look at the coin.
7. While you are looking at the coin, ask your helper to tape the card to the far wall of the second room so that

the line on the card and the bottom of the coin line up.

8. As you look at the coin, slowly walk toward the X until you are standing on the tape directly beneath the coin. As you walk, notice how the bottom of the coin lines up with the card, wall, or ceiling.

Results The coin appears to rise above the horizon line on the card as you walk toward the X.

Why? The height of the coin above the horizon, like the altitude of Polaris, depends on your latitude when viewing it. In this experiment the tape marked X represents the North Pole; the tape marked E, the equator; the coin, Polaris; and the line on the card, the horizon. As you move from the E toward the X, the height of the coin above the horizon line increases until, at the X, the coin is directly overhead. As in this experiment, if one could move quickly from the equator to the North Pole, the location of Polaris would first seem to be at the horizon and then appear to move above the horizon until it is directly overhead.

24. In Line

Purpose To prepare a model of an optical double star.

Materials 2 index cards   scissors
pencil   yardstick (meterstick)

Procedure

1. Fold each card in half, placing the short sides together. Unfold the cards.
2. On one of the cards, draw a star large enough to cover half of the card. Draw a dashed line around the star as shown in the diagram.
3. Place the two cards together and cut out the star in both cards by cutting along the dashed line. Make sure to cut through both layers of paper.
4. Separate the cards and label them by writing 1 on one star and 2 on the other star.
5. Bend the cards along the fold line so that the stars stand up when the uncut half of the card is placed on a flat surface.
6. Lay the measuring stick on a table so that the zero end is near the edge of the table and facing you. Stand star 1 on the zero end of the measuring stick and star 2 on the opposite end of the stick.
7. Look at the stars at eye level, positioning yourself directly in front of star 1. Move your head to the left until you are able to see most of star 2.

Results When viewed from a position directly in front of the stars, star 1 blocks your view of star 2. Both stars are seen when viewed from an angle, and they appear to be close together.

Why? When you are in front of the nearest star, it blocks your view of the star behind it. Looking at the stars from a slight angle allows both stars to be seen. The stars appear close to each other because they are in the same line of sight. The paper stars are models of an **optical double,** two stars that appear to be close together but are not physically near each other and have no relationship to each other. In the Big Dipper, the stars Mizar and Alcor are an optical double.

25. Spreading

Purpose   To demonstrate how a star's distance affects its apparent magnitude.

Materials   2 identical incandescent flashlights with new batteries
yardstick (meterstick)
2 helpers

NOTE: This experiment must be performed outdoors after dark.

Procedure

1. Ask your helpers to stand side by side.
2. Turn the flashlights on and have each helper hold one.
3. Stand about 10 feet (3 m) in front of your helpers.
4. Instruct your helpers to point the lights toward your face.
5. Look at the lights just long enough to compare their brightness. Do not stare at the lights.
6. Ask one of your helpers to move about 30 feet (9 m) or more from you while continuing to point the light toward you.
7. Again, compare the brightness of the lights.

Results   The brightness of the lights appears to be the same when they are at the same distance from you. When they are at different distances, the closer light looks brighter.

Why?   The light from the flashlights represents the light from two stars that give off the same amount of light. The light spreads out uniformly in all directions from the flashlights, as it does from stars. The spreading of light from more distant stars results in less light reaching Earth. Thus, two stars that give off the same amount of light, but are at different distances from Earth, will appear to have different **apparent magnitudes** (a measure of how bright a celestial body appears to be).

26. Cover-Up

Purpose   To demonstrate an eclipsing binary system.

Materials   drawing compass
ruler
sheet of typing paper
2 pencils
scissors
transparent tape

Procedure

1. Use the compass to draw a 2-inch (5-cm) and a 4-inch (10-cm) circle on the paper.
2. Write A on the smaller circle and B on the larger circle.
3. Use a pencil to color the larger circle.
4. Cut out the circles, then tape a circle to the sharpened end of each pencil.
5. Hold the pencil with circle A upright about 6 to 8 inches (15 to 20 cm) in front of your face.
6. Hold the pencil with circle B upside down about 4 inches (10 cm) behind circle A.
7. Observe how much of each circle is visible.
8. Move circle B around and in front of circle A.
9. Observe the visibility of each circle during this movement.

Results   When circle B is behind circle A, all of A and part of B are visible. As circle B moves around, both circles are visible for a short time, then B covers A.

Why?   The circles represent two stars, one of which is smaller and brighter than the other. The positions of these two stars are such that, seen from Earth, one of the stars eclipses the other. Both stars revolve around a common point (although only the orbit of the larger star is demonstrated here). This kind of star pair is called an **eclipsing binary system**. The eclipse of star B by star A is represented by moving circle B behind circle A. The eclipse of star A by star B is represented by moving circle A behind circle B. When the two stars are not in eclipse, the light from both is seen, so the stars look brighter.

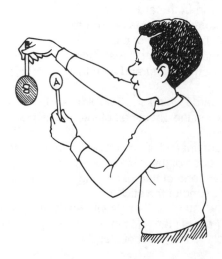

27. Brighter

Purpose To demonstrate how refractive telescopes make celestial bodies more visible.

Materials 2 sheets of typing paper
transparent tape
ruler
measuring cup
2 cups (500 ml) rice
2 large bowls
helper

Procedure

1. Roll each paper into a cone and secure with tape. Make one cone about 1 inch (2.5 cm) in diameter across the opening, and the other about 6 inches (15 cm) in diameter.
2. Place 1 cup (250 ml) of rice in one of the large bowls.
3. Set the empty bowl on the ground outdoors. A grassy area works well.
4. Ask your helper to hold the smaller cone, open end up, in the empty bowl.
5. Holding the bowl of rice about 3 feet (1 m) above the opening in the cone, pour the rice into the cone.
6. Use the measuring cup to measure the amount of rice that falls into the cone.
7. Repeat steps 2 through 6, using the larger cone.

Results More rice is caught by the larger cone.

Why? Refractive telescopes used to study the stars have one large end and one small end. The large end, directed toward the sky, has an objective lens that collects large quantities of light, just as the large cone collects large quantities of rice. The small end of the telescope has an eyepiece. This second lens magnifies the images received by the objective lens. Larger objective lenses collect more light and produce brighter images of the celestial bodies being observed.

28. Light Out

Purpose To construct an astronomer's flashlight.

Materials rule
scissors
red transparent report folder
flashlight
rubber band

Procedure

1. Cut a 4-by-8-inch (10-by-20-cm) strip from the red folder.
2. Fold the strip in half to form a 4-inch (10-cm) square.
3. Cover the end of the flashlight with the square and secure with the rubber band.
4. Use the flashlight to read this book outdoors at night.

NOTE: Keep the instrument for Experiment 31, "Star Finder."

Results An astronomer's flashlight is constructed.

Why? When you move from a lighted area to a dark area, at first you can hardly see. After a few minutes, changes occur in your eyes and you see better. In about 30 minutes to 1 hour, the changes are complete and your vision is even better. Although your vision is not as good as in the light, it is the best it will be in the dark. You now have **night vision** (ability to see in the dark).

One flash of white light can reverse the changes in the eye, causing you to lose your night vision. It takes another 30 to 60 minutes or so to get it back again. Red light affects night vision less than does white light, so the astronomer's flashlight is covered with a red filter. You can use it to read a star map and still see the stars in the sky.

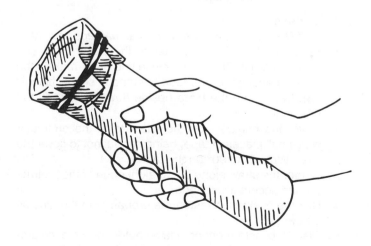

29. Light Separator

Purpose To model how astronomers study the makeup of stars.

Materials compact disc (CD)

Procedure
CAUTION: Never look directly at the Sun or reflect its light to your eyes. It can damage your eyes.
1. Hold the compact disc so that sunlight coming through a window hits its shiny side.
2. Move the disc back and forth several times.
3. Observe the color patterns on the disc.

Results Bands of color are seen on the disc.

Why? The disc behaves like a **spectroscope,** an instrument that separates visible light into a **spectrum** (a band of colored lights). The colors on the disc appear to be a **continuous spectrum,** which means its colors are arranged in continuous order. The order of the colors seen is red, orange, yellow, green, blue, indigo, and violet. With a more precise instrument, such as a spectroscope, the Sun's spectrum is seen as a **dark-line spectrum** (a continuous spectrum crossed by dark lines). The placement of the dark lines gives astronomers clues they use to discover the types of **elements** (substances made up of chemically identical particles) that make up the Sun or any star observed through a spectroscope.

30. Star Heights

Purpose To construct an astrolabe.

Materials
cardboard tube from a paper towel roll	protractor
paper plate	marking pen
pencil	drinking straw
scissors	pushpin
masking tape	helper

Procedure
CAUTION: Do not look at the Sun. It can damage your eyes.
1. Stand the tube in the center of the paper plate and draw around it. Cut out the circle you drew, making the hole big enough for the tube to stand in snugly but still turn freely. Turn the plate upside down and stand the tube in the hole.
2. Cover the numbers on the left side of the protractor with small pieces of tape, being careful not to cover the lines. Write 0° to 90° on the tape.
3. Center the straw along the straight edge of the protractor and secure it with tape.
4. Use the pushpin to fasten the protractor to the tube as shown.
5. Place the instrument on a table outdoors. Hold the protractor so that the straw is perpendicular to the tube. Point the straw toward the horizon in any direction.
6. Close one eye and look through the straw with your open eye. If you cannot see the horizon through the straw, then adjust the height of the protractor on the tube.
7. Ask your helper to mark an arrow on the tube below the 0° mark taped on the protractor.
8. Look through the straw again at an object above the horizon. Note the position of the straw and the angle indicated by the arrow on the tube.
NOTE: Keep the instrument for the next experiment.

Results You have made an astrolabe.

Why? An **astrolabe** is an instrument used to measure the altitude of celestial bodies, such as stars. Altitude is the angular distance of the star above the horizon. The straw of the astrolabe made in this experiment first points toward the horizon, which has an altitude of 0°. When you raise the end of the straw in order to see an object above the horizon, the protractor rotates on the pushpin. As the end of the protractor rotates upward, the arrow on the tube indicates increasingly greater angles.

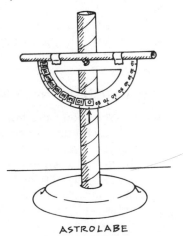

ASTROLABE

31. Star Finder

Purpose To measure the azimuth and altitude of a star.

Materials
astrolabe from
Experiment 30,
"Star Heights"
protractor
pen
directional compass

masking tape
astronomer's flashlight
from Experiment 28,
"Light Out"
helper

Procedure

1. Remove the paper plate from the astrolabe. Construct a compass rose by using the second protractor and the pen to mark every 10° clockwise around the edge of the plate as shown, starting with 0°. Label 0°N, 90°E, 189°S, and 270°W. Reassemble the astrolabe.

2. At night, go outdoors and place the astrolabe on the edge of a table. Use the compass to position the compass rose so that 0° points due north.

3. Tape the compass rose to the table in this position.

4. Holding the end of the straw that is near you and keeping one eye closed, look through the straw and search for a star. Slowly push down on the end of the straw to see above the horizon, and rotate the tube to search horizontally.

5. Ask your helper to use the flashlight first to read the angle on the protractor as indicated by the arrow on the tube and then to look at the compass rose to determine the direction the straw is pointing.

6. Repeat steps 4 and 5 locating several stars within a single constellation.

Results The higher the selected star is above the horizon, the greater the angle. As the tube is turned, the astrolabe points to a different part of the horizon.

Why? As the end of the protractor rotates upward, the arrow on the tube points to an angle on the protractor. This angle is the altitude of the star being observed. As the tube is rotated, the straw points to an angle on the **compass rose** (a circle divided into 360° numbered clockwise from due north). This angle is the star's **azimuth** (the distance of an object, such as a star or any celestial body, in degrees clockwise around the horizon from due north).

---

32. The Dark Trail

Purpose To demonstrate why a nebula has dark areas.

Materials
one-hole paper punch
index card
ruler

transparent tape
pencil

Procedure

1. Punch 2 holes in the index card as shown.

2. Tear off a piece of tape about 1 inch (2.5 cm) long and place it over one of the holes.

3. Face an open window that does not have direct sunlight.

4. Close one eye, and hold the card in front of your open eye. Look through each hole and observe the amount of light that you can see through the holes.
CAUTION: Never look directly at the Sun. It can damage your eyes.

5. Tear off a second piece of tape about 1½ inches (3.75 cm) long. Stick one end of the tape next to the covered hole. Loop the tape over the hole by supporting it with the point of the pencil and attaching the other end to the opposite side of the hole as shown. Remove the pencil.

6. Again, look through the holes in the card, observing the amount of light you can see through each hole.

7. Repeat steps 5 and 6 five times, increasing the length of tape by about ½ inch (1.25 cm) each time and attaching each loop over the preceding one. The loops should not stick to each other.

Results The amount of light coming through the uncovered hole does not change. but the light coming through the covered hole decreases as each piece of tape is added, until little or no light can be seen.

Why? Interstellar dust is small particles of matter between celestial bodies. A **nebula** is a cloud of interstellar dust and gas spread across many millions of miles (kilometers) in space. Like a nebula, the clear plastic tape in this experiment is **transparent,** meaning that light passes straight through it. One's view changes slightly when looking through single or even double layers of transparent materials. But as the layers of transparent material separated by layers of air increase, more and more light is blocked. The same thing is true when looking through a nebula made of clouds of dust and gas. The dark areas in the nebula are due to interstellar materials that block light.

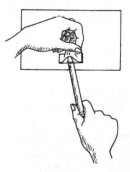

33. Dirty Snowball

Purpose To make a scale model of a comet.

Materials large white cotton ball
ruler
school glue
¼ teaspoon (1.25 ml) soil
2 rolls of crepe paper—
1 blue, 1 white
scissors
yardstick
(meterstick)
masking tape
adult helper

Procedure
1. Unroll the cotton ball and spread it to form a piece about 3 × 3 inches (7.5 × 7.5 cm).
2. Pull a dime-size piece off one corner of the cotton. Roll this piece of cotton into a ball.
3. Place 8 to 10 dots of glue on the cotton, then sprinkle it with soil.
4. Place the dirty cotton ball in the center of the cotton. Wrap the cotton around the ball to make a large ball about 1 inch (2.5 cm) in diameter. Place 20 to 25 dots of glue on the outside of this cotton ball, then sprinkle it with soil. This large ball represents the head of a comet.
5. Using the blue crepe paper, cut three or more 6-foot (1.8-m) strips. Repeat, using the white crepe paper.
6. Stack the blue strips on top of the white strips and glue their ends together. These colored strips represent the two tails of a comet. Glue the comet head to the glued end of the tails.
7. Allow the glue to dry. This should take 15 to 30 minutes.

8. Ask an adult to tape the comet's head to the wall, at least 6 feet (1.8 m) above the floor.

NOTE: Keep the model for the next experiment.

Results A comet is modeled.

Why? A **comet** is a small celestial body made up of interstellar dust and gases that revolves around the Sun. A comet consists of a head and, often, two tails. The head, which has been described as a dirty snowball, has a central **nucleus** surrounded by a large layer of dust and gases, called a **coma.** In the model, the small, compact, dirty cotton ball represents the nucleus and the large, fluffier, dirty cotton ball represents the coma. The two tails are represented by strips of blue and white crepe paper. (For information about the tails, see the next experiment.)

The scale of the comet model is 1 inch (2.5 cm) = 30,000 miles (48,000 km). Thus, the comet's head has a diameter of 30,000 miles (48,000 km) and the tails are 2.16 million miles (3.46 million km) long. While comets are different sizes, this model represents an average-size comet.

---

34. Fly Away

Purpose To model the two kinds of comet tails.

Materials comet model from Experiment 33, "Dirty Snowball"
masking tape
drawing compass
ruler
yellow construction paper
scissors

Procedure
1. Keep the comet model taped to the wall as described in "Dirty Snowball." Allow the blue paper strips to hang straight down, but tape the white strips to the wall so they curve to one side.
2. Draw an 8-inch (20-cm)-diameter circle on the yellow paper. Cut out the circle. Label the circle SUN.
3. Tape the yellow circle above the comet's head on the wall.

Results The crepe paper strips stream out away from the Sun.

Why? The crepe paper "tails" represent two tails from a comet's coma. An **astronomical unit** (AU) is the distance from Earth to the Sun. If a comet gets within 2 AU of the Sun, gases and interstellar dust from the comet are blown outward by **solar wind** (an energetic stream of charged particles constantly moving away from the Sun). A comet's

tail always points away from the Sun, whether it is moving toward the Sun or away from it. Often two tails form. One, called an **ion tail,** is composed of gases that are **ionized** (electrically charged) by solar wind. The charged gases glow with a blue color, as represented by the blue crepe paper. The other is a **dust tail** and is made of dust that glows white because it reflects sunlight, as shown by the white paper. The charged gases in the ion tail follow the charged particles of the solar wind away from the Sun, and the heavier dust particles in the dust tail generally remain in the orbit of the comet around the Sun, giving the dust tail a curved shape.

35. Circling

Purpose To demonstrate the path of a satellite.

Materials
cookie sheet with
   raised sides
cardboard tube from a
   toilet tissue roll
masking tape
sheet of office paper

cup
tap water
red food coloring
spoon
marble
modeling clay

Procedure

1. Lay the cookie sheet on a table. Place the cardboard tube in one corner of the cookie sheet so that one end of the tube rests on the rim of one short side of the pan. Secure the raised end of the tube to the rim of the pan with tape.
2. Lay the paper in the pan so that the untaped end of the tube rests on the edge of the paper.
3. Fill the cup about one-fourth full with water and add 10 drops of food coloring. Stir.
4. Wet the marble with the colored water, place it in the elevated end of the tube, and release it.
5. Prop up the long side of the pan nearer the tube about 1 inch (2.5 cm) by placing 2 lumps of clay under both corners of the long side.
6. Again, wet the marble, place it in the tube, and release it.

Results Spots of red water mark the two paths of the marble. The path across the level pan is straight, while the path across the raised pan is curved.

Why? A **satellite** is a body in orbit around a celestial body. This includes natural satellites, such as moons orbiting **planets** (celestial bodies that orbit the Sun), as well as man-made satellites, such as weather satellites orbiting Earth. Satellites, like the marble in this experiment, are acted on by two **forces** (cause a change in motion) that are produced by forward motion and gravity. **Gravity** is the force of **attraction** (a force that draws things together) between two bodies. The gravity of the celestial body that the satellite is orbiting exerts a downward pull on the satellite. Forward motion and gravity keep the satellite in orbit. The path of a satellite, like that of the marble on the elevated pan, curves because its forward speed and the planet's gravity pull the satellite down toward the planet. Without gravity, satellites would move in a straight path, and without forward speed, gravity would pull the satellite into the planet.

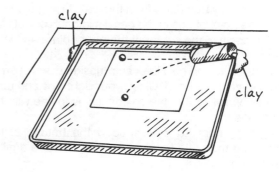

36. Lineup

Purpose To make a model that shows what people in the past thought the universe looked like.

Materials
yardstick
22-by-28-inch (55-by-70-cm) piece of
   poster board
pencil
26-inch (65-cm) piece of string
school glue
8 Styrofoam craft balls
15–20 gummed stars

Procedure

1. Lay the yardstick (meterstick) lengthwise across the center of the poster board.
2. Beginning from the left edge of the poster board, measure and mark 9 small dots, one every 3 inches (7.5 cm), along the center of the board. The last dot will be 1 inch (2.5 cm) from the right edge.
3. Tie a loop in one end of the string.
4. Insert the pencil point through the loop and place the point on the second dot from the left side of the paper. Pull the string back over the first dot and hold the string on this dot with your thumb. Using the pencil and string as a drawing compass, draw as much of a circle as possible by moving the pencil across the poster board on both sides of the second dot.
5. Repeat step 4 for each of the other dots, holding the string on the first dot each time.

6. Glue one Styrofoam ball to each of the first 8 dots.
7. Using the marking pen, add labels as shown.
8. Draw the stars in the space beyond Saturn.

Results You have made a model that shows how people in the past thought the universe was organized.

Why? In this experiment, a **geocentric** (Earth-centered) model of the universe is made. This model was proposed by the ancient astronomer Ptolemy, who lived and worked in Alexandria, Greece, about A.D. 140. Ptolemy believed that Earth was motionless and that the Moon, the planets, and the Sun revolved around Earth. An outer dome of stars was thought to exist beyond the farthest planet (then thought to be Saturn). In comparison to the stars, the Moon and the Sun did not wander in their paths, but the other celestial bodies did. Thus, these were called "planets" from the Greek word for wanderers. Today's model of the solar system is **heliocentric** (Sun-centered) and has nine planets.

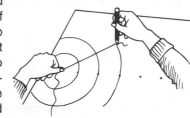

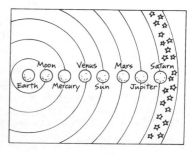

37. Back and Forth

Purpose To learn why the inferior planets sometimes appear to go backward as seen from Earth.

Materials
2-yard (2-m) strip of adding-machine paper
black marker
yardstick (meterstick)
transparent tape
chair
2 pencils
grape-size ball of modeling clay
paper plate
writing paper
helper

Procedure

1. Place the strip of paper on a table. At the edge of the left end of the strip, draw a large star. Draw 13 stars, 6 inches (15 cm) apart, and number the stars from left to right.
2. Use tape to secure the strip to the wall 1 yard (1 m) above the floor and parallel to the floor.
3. Set a chair 2 yards (2 m) from the wall, facing the strip.
4. Insert the point of one of the pencils into the ball of clay.
5. Draw a circle in the center of the paper plate and label it Sun.
6. Sit in the chair and hold the pencil upside down at arm's length in your left hand. Close your right eye and position the pencil so that the ball of clay is in line with the center star.
7. Using your right hand to support the bottom of the plate, hold the plate horizontally with its edge against the clay ball.
8. Slowly move the clay ball in a counterclockwise direction around the plate. As the ball moves, call out each of the star numbers that the clay ball passes in front of. Ask your helper to record these numbers. Stop when the ball is in front of the plate and again in line with the center star.

Results At first, the recorded numbers get lower, then the same number is repeated several times before the numbers get higher.

Why? The clay ball represents one of the **inferior planets** (the planets Mercury and Venus, which are in orbit between Earth and the Sun), the paper plate is the planet's orbital path around the Sun, and you are an observer on Earth. The star numbers are place markers on the orbital path. As an inferior planet moves around its orbit, as seen from Earth, it appears at times to move forward in relationship to the stars, indicated by the lower star numbers. But then the planet seems to stop, indicated by the repeated star number, and then moves backward, indicated by the higher star numbers. This apparent backward motion of a planet in relation to the stars is called **retrograde motion**. Actually, inferior planets, like the ball, are not moving back and forth in the sky, but are moving around the Sun in their orbit. They appear to move forward (eastward) when they are on the side of the orbit farthest from Earth and backward (westward) when on the side closest to Earth. When the planets move toward or away from Earth, they appear not to be moving at all. Note that unlike the ball, the inferior planets are not visible from Earth throughout their orbit because the Sun blocks the view of these planets.

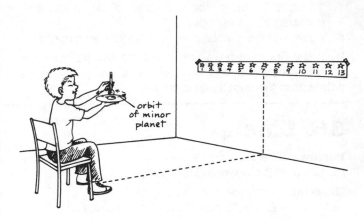

orbit of minor planet

38. Planet Size

Purpose To use models to compare the size of Mercury and Earth.

Materials
12-by-12-inch (30-by-30-cm) piece of white poster board
drawing compass
metric ruler
scissors
pencil

Procedure

1. On the poster board, draw several circles, each with a 3-cm diameter.
2. Cut out the circles and label each one M for Mercury.
3. Make a circle with an 8-cm diameter. Label the circle E for Earth.
4. Lay the large circle on a table. Place the smaller circles across the middle of the large circle to determine how many Mercurys will fit cross Earth's diameter.

Results The number of Mercurys that fit across Earth's diameter is about 2⅔.

Why? Earth's **equatorial diameter** (diameter at the equator) is about 8,000 miles (12,800 km). Mercury's equatorial diameter is about 3,000 miles (4,800 km). In this experiment, models of Earth and Mercury are made to a scale of 1 cm = 1,000 miles (1,600 km). Thus, the model of Earth has a diameter of 8 cm and that of Mercury, 3 cm. It takes about 2⅔ Mercury models to cover the Earth model's diameter. Thus, Earth's diameter is about 2⅔ times greater than Mercury's diameter.

39. Together

Purpose To make scale models of Earth and the Moon.

Materials two 5-by-8-inch (12.5-by-20-cm) unruled index cards
drawing compass
metric ruler
pen

Procedure

1. The diameter of the Moon is 3,476 km. Using a scale of 1 cm = 2,000 km, the diameter of the Moon model would be calculated as follows:

$$\frac{\text{Moon's real}}{\text{diameter}} \div 2{,}000 \text{ km/cm} = \frac{\text{Moon model's}}{\text{diameter}}$$

$$3{,}476 \text{ km} \div 2{,}000 \text{ km/cm} = 1.738 \text{ cm}$$

Rounding the number off to the nearest tenth of a cm, the Moon model's diameter would be 1.7 cm.

2. Fold one of the index cards in half by placing the short ends together. Use the compass to draw a 1.7-cm diameter circle on one side of the folded card.

3. Use the ruler and pen to label this card Moon and label the diameter of the circle 3,476 km, as shown.

4. Repeat steps 1 through 3 to make a scale model of Earth on the other index card. Use 12,756 km for Earth's diameter.

5. Stand the index cards on a table so that the Moon and Earth models are next to each other. How do their sizes compare?

Results Scale models of Earth and the Moon are made and compared.

Why? The name Moon has been given to the natural satellite of Earth. But other planets also have moons. The Moon model in this experiment is called a scale model because it is smaller than the real object by a specific amount. The scale used was 1 cm = 2,000 km. Since the Moon has a diameter of 3,476 km, the diameter of the Moon's scale model is 3,476 ÷ 2,000 = 1.7 cm. Earth has a diameter of 12,756 km, thus the diameter of Earth's scale model is 12,756 ÷ 2,000 = 6.4 cm. Earth is almost four times bigger than the Moon.

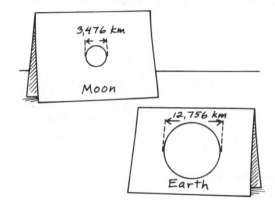

40. How Cold?

Purpose To model how distance from the Sun affects the amount of solar energy a planet receives.

Materials transparent tape
sheet of graph paper
ruler
flashlight
felt-tipped pen
helper

Procedure

1. Tape the graph paper to a wall at chest height.

2. Hold the end of the ruler perpendicular to the center of the graph paper.

3. Using the ruler as a guide, hold the flashlight ½ inch (1.25 cm) in front of the graph paper.

4. As your helper to use the pen to trace around the outside circle of light on the paper.

5. Move the light 2 inches (5 cm) from the paper and repeat step 4.

Result The circle of light is larger when the light is farther from the paper.

Why? Light leaving the flashlight spreads out just as light leaving most light sources does, including the Sun. Since the same amount of light left the flashlight, the smaller circle of light indicated a more **concentrated** (gathered closely together) amount of light. Light is a form of **energy** (the ability to cause changes in matter). Thus, more energy was received in the small lighted area when the flashlight was closer to the paper. **Solar energy** is **radiation** (energy in the form of rays or waves) from the Sun. Solar energy is a combination of different kinds of energy, including visible light energy and infrared energy (heat). The farther a planet is from the Sun, the less concentrated the solar energy it receives. The amount of solar energy received affects a planet's temperature. Generally, the temperature of a planet decreases with distance from the Sun.

II
Biology

pinecone

seeds on inside of scale

41. Soaker

Purpose To show how plants help moisten soil.

Materials ruler
masking tape
two 7-ounce (210-ml) plastic drinking cups
marking pen
potting soil
3 craft sticks
tap water
timer

Procedure

1. Place a 2-inch (5-cm) piece of tape on the side of each cup so that one end of the tape touches the rim of the cup.
2. Make a mark on the tape ½ inch (1.25 cm) from the top of the cup.
3. Pack soil into the cups up to the bottom edge of the tape.
4. Move each craft stick back and forth slightly as you insert the 3 sticks into the soil of one cup.
5. Add water up to the mark in each cup, and then mark the height again after 1 minute.

Results The height of the water in the cup with the craft sticks is lower than that in the cup without the sticks.

Why? When water is added to the cup with the sticks, the water runs into the openings the sticks make in the soil. The growing roots of plants, like the sticks, make tiny openings as they move through the soil. This allows rainwater to fill the openings and soak into the soil instead of running over its surface. Water that soaks into the soil can be used by plants.

water

soil

42. Attractive

Purpose To determine how water affects seeds.

Materials ½ cup (125 ml) dry pinto beans
clear plastic 2-cup (500-ml) measuring cup
tap water
timer

Procedure

1. Place the beans in the cup.
2. Add enough water to the cup to cover the beans.
3. Observe and record the volume (amount of space taken up) of the beans in the cup.
4. Allow the beans to sit undisturbed for 24 hours.
5. After 24 hours, observe and record the volume of the beans. Discard the beans.

Results After 24 hours, the volume of the beans has increased. Little or no water is left in the cup.

Why? The volume of the beans increases while the volume of water decreases because the water moves into the beans. The beans are **hydrophilic,** meaning they have an attraction for water. The beans are also **porous,** meaning they contain many tiny holes that water can pass through. The process by which a hydrophilic, porous material **absorbs** (takes in) water is called **imbibition.** When dry seeds, such as the beans, are watered, they **imbibe** (absorb) water and swell.

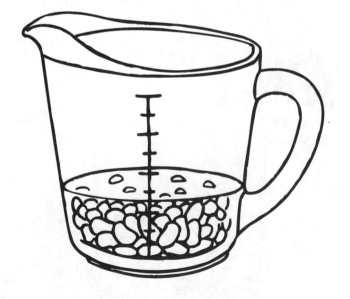

43. Outside

Purpose To determine what's on the outside of a pinto bean.

Materials 4 to 5 dry pinto beans
coffee cup
ruler
tap water
timer
paper towel

Procedure

1. Place the beans in the cup and cover them with about 2 inches (5 cm) of water.
2. Soak the beans for 24 hours.
3. After 24 hours, take the beans out of the cup and place them on the paper towel to absorb the excess water.
4. Inspect the outside of the beans. Use your fingernails to remove and examine part of the outer covering from one of the beans.

NOTE: Keep two of the remaining beans for the next experiment.

Results The outside of the pinto bean consists of a brown outer coating and a light-colored, oval-shaped scar. The outer covering is thin and peels off easily.

Why? Beans are seeds that grow inside a casing called a **pod.** The outer covering of a seed is called the **seed coat.** The seed coat helps protect the inside of the seed from insects, disease, and damage. The scar on the seed coat is the **hilum** (the place where the seed was attached to the pod).

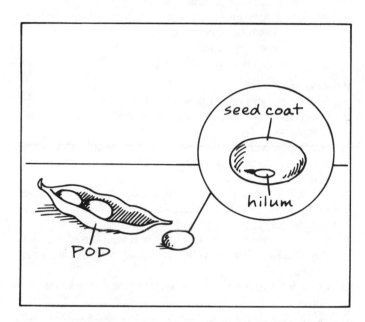

44. Under

Purpose To identify the parts under the seed coat of a pinto bean.

Materials soaked beans from Experiment 43, "Outside"
magnifying lens

Procedure

1. Use your fingernails to peel the seed coat off one of the soaked beans.
2. Use the magnifying lens to inspect the outside of the peeled bean. Find the parts identified in the figure.
3. Separate the bean into two halves.
4. Find the parts identified in the figure.
5. Repeat steps 1 through 4 with the remaining beans if parts of the first bean are broken during handling.

Results Beneath the seed coat is a white structure with two halves connected at a single spot at the top. At the point of connection is a beak-shaped structure. Inside is a leaflike structure.

Why? The two halves of the bean are **cotyledons,** or seed leaves, which are simple leaves that store food for the developing plant **embryo** (an organism in its earliest stages of development) inside the seed. The beak-shaped structure extending from the point of connection is called the **hypocotyl.** The hypocotyl is the part of the plant embryo that develops into the lower stem and root. The tip of the hypocotyl, called the **radicle,** develops into roots. Inside the bean is the **epicotyl,** the part of the embryo located above the hypocotyl. The epicotyl develops into the plant's stem, leaves, flowers, and fruit. The tiny immature leaves at the end of the epicotyl are called the **plumule,** which develop into the first true leaves.

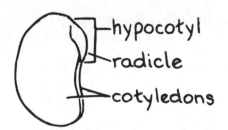

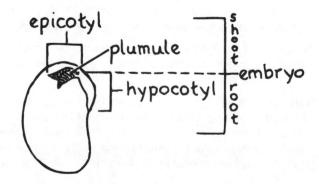

45. Hidden

Purpose To determine the location of seeds in a pinecone.

Materials several sheets of newspaper
2 old washcloths
3 to 5 immature pinecones (small pinecones with tightly closed scales)
timer (optional)
adult helper

Procedure

1. Spread out the newspaper on a table.
2. Wrap a washcloth around each end of one of the pinecones.
3. Holding a washcloth-covered end in each hand, twist the cone back and forth several times to loosen its scales.

NOTE: If it is too difficult to twist the cone, soak all of the cones in water for 2 to 3 hours. Ask an adult for help if it is still too difficult to twist the cone.

4. While holding the base of the cone with the cloth, use the fingers of your other hand to pull out several scales.
5. Look for two seeds on the inside of each scale, as shown.

NOTE: If you do not find seeds, repeat steps 2 to 4 with another pinecone.

Results Two seeds, each attached to a paperlike wing, are found on the inside of the scales of the pinecone, hidden from view.

Why? The pinecone contains the seeds of a pine tree. Pine trees are **conifers,** nonflowering plants that reproduce by forming cones. Most conifers are **evergreen** (having leaves that remain green all through the year) trees with small needle-shaped leaves and two types of cones. One is a small cone, called the **pollen cone,** which contains pollen and forms in groups at the tip of a branch. The other is a larger **seed cone,** which contains seeds and usually forms as a single cone away from the tip of a branch.

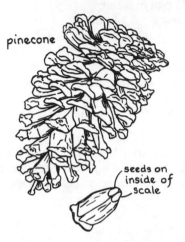

pinecone

seeds on inside of scale

---

46. Lights Out!

Purpose To determine how light affects the color of grass.

Materials medium-size cooking pot or metal bowl
area of short grass
1 quart (1 liter) water (optional)

Procedure

NOTE: This experiment causes temporary yellow patches on the grass. You must get an adult's approval to perform the experiment.

1. Place the pot, open end down, on an area of green grass.

NOTE: If the soil is very dry, pour water over the grass before placing the pot on it.

2. Allow the pot to sit undisturbed for 10 days.
3. At the end of 10 days, remove the pot. Compare the color of the grass that was beneath the pot with the color of the grass around the area that was covered.

Results After 10 days, the grass covered by the pot has turned from green to yellow. The grass around the covered area remains green.

Why? Plants like grass are green because of a green **pigment** (coloring substance) called **chlorophyll.** The part of a plant cell where chlorophyll is found and where food is made is called a **chloroplast.** Light is necessary for chlorophyll to develop in the chloroplasts. Without light, chemical changes in the chloroplasts cause chlorophyll to break down faster than it is made. The chloroplasts contain mainly chlorophyll, but they also contain other pigments, such as pale yellow pigments called **xanthophyll** and yellow or orange pigments called **carotene.** When chlorophyll breaks down, the yellow pigments in the grass, like those in any plant, are exposed and the plant looks yellow. The loss of green color in plants is called **chlorosis.**

47. Protector

Purpose To model how organisms block the Sun's rays.

Materials pencil
4-by-4-inch (10-by-10-cm) square of poster board
scissors
sheet of red construction paper
transparent tape
timer

Procedure

1. Draw a shape, such as a star, as large as possible on the poster board. Cut out the shape.
2. Place the poster board shape in the center of the red sheet of paper. Tape the edges of the shape to the paper to hold the shape in place.
3. On a window that receives direct sunlight, tape the red paper to the window so that the poster board shape is against the window.
4. After 24 or more hours, remove the paper from the window.
5. Carefully remove the poster board shape from the paper.
6. Compare the color of the area of paper that was covered by the shape with the color of the uncovered area.

Results The paper is darker where it was covered by the paper shape and lighter when it was not covered.

Why? The poster board is **opaque** (doesn't allow light to pass through). Thus, the poster board acts as a sunblock, absorbing sunlight, thus preventing the light from reaching the paper that the poster board covers. Pigments in living organisms, such as melanin in human skin, protect organisms by absorbing **ultraviolet light,** or **UVL** (light from the Sun that in excess can be dangerous to humans or other life-forms). It is believed that antarctic **phytoplankton** (small, often microscopic, plantlike water-dwelling organisms that are capable of using light to produce food) may have the capacity to adapt to increased amounts of UVL by producing their own sunblock pigments.

48. Shady

Purpose To determine how distance from a light source affects the amount of light received by a plant.

Materials scissors
roll of wide paper with no designs, such as butcher paper
small houseplant about 12 inches (30 cm) tall
flashlight
yardstick (meterstick)
3 crayons of different colors
helper

Procedure

1. Cut a square of paper that is about twice as wide as the widest part of the plant.
2. Place the paper on the floor and set the plant in the center of the paper.
3. Darken the room and hold the flashlight just above the plant.
4. Ask a helper to use one of the crayons to outline the plant's shadow on the paper.
5. Move the flashlight to about 1 foot (3 m) above the plant.
6. Ask your helper to outline the shadow on the paper with a crayon of a different color.
7. Move the flashlight to about 2 feet (6 m) above the plant.
8. Again, have your helper outline the shadow on the paper with the remaining crayon.

Results The shadow is smaller when the light is held farther above the plant.

Why? The plant blocks the light coming from the flashlight. The size of the plant's shadow indicates how much light the plant blocks, and thus indicates how much light reaches the plant. A plant closer to a light casts a larger shadow and receives more light than a plant that is farther away from the light and casts a smaller shadow.

49. With and Without

Purpose To determine if light on the soil is needed for mustard seed germination.

Materials pencil   mustard seeds
3 egg cartons (poly-   1-tablespoon (15-ml)
  styrene, not paper)   measuring spoon
scissors   tap water
3 cups (750 ml) potting soil

Procedure

1. Use the following steps to construct a closable germinating tray:
   - Use the pencil to punch a small drainage hole in the bottom of each compartment of one of the egg cartons.
   - Cut the lid off a second carton. Discard the bottom of the carton. *NOTE: Recycle discarded polystyrene.*
   - Set the first egg carton in the lid of the second carton so that the lid will catch water draining through the holes.
2. Construct an open germinating tray, using the third egg carton. Repeat the previous procedure, but remove the lid from the egg carton and use that lid to collect drainage water.
3. Fill the compartments of both germinating trays about half full with soil.
4. Sprinkle a few mustard seeds in each compartment of the trays.
5. Cover the seeds with about 1 tablespoon (15 ml) of soil.
6. Moisten the soil in each tray with an equal amount of water. Keep the soil in each tray moist, but not wet, during the entire experiment.

7. Close the lid of the first germinating tray. Place both trays near a window that receives light most of the day, such as a window facing south.
8. Observe the open tray daily for the first signs of plant growth.

Results The seeds in both trays germinate.

Why? During the last stages of seed development, the seed **dehydrates** (loses water) until it contains very little water. The embryo ceases to grow and remains inactive until the seed **germinates** (begins to grow). Thus, germination doesn't mean that a seed comes alive, but rather that it resumes the growth and development that stopped during the last stages of seed development.

Some seeds, such as mustard, germinate as soon as they are in favorable conditions. Favorable conditions for mustard seeds are sufficient warmth, water, and oxygen. All the seeds in this experiment were exposed to light before being planted. Since the seeds grew in the closed tray, light on the soil was not needed for the seeds to germinate.

---

50. Stored

Purpose To determine where carrots store their food.

Materials 1-quart (1-liter) jar
tap water
blue food coloring
carrot with leaves

Procedure

1. Fill the jar about one-fourth full with water.
2. Add enough food coloring to make the water a deep blue color.
3. Use your fingers to break the tip off the carrot's end, then stand the carrot in the jar of colored water.
4. After 2 days or more, remove the carrot from the water and break it into four equal parts.
5. Observe the surface of each cross section.

Results The cross sections have a light orange area surrounding a blue center.

Why? The carrot that you eat is a root. The center of this root contains **xylem tubes,** which transport sap containing water and dissolved minerals from the soil up into the rest

of the carrot plant. In this experiment, the water contains blue coloring, thus the xylem tubes are colored blue. The area around the root's center contains **phloem tubes,** which transport sap containing water and food manufactured in the plant's leaves throughout the plant and down to the root where they are stored.

51. Changes

Purpose To demonstrate how environment changed the body temperature of dinosaurs.

Materials

unruled index card	thermometer
pencil	writing paper
scissors	timer
ruler	adult helper

Procedure

1. Fold the index card in half lengthwise.
2. Draw a dinosaur on one side of the folded card.
3. Ask an adult to cut two slits in the center of the other side of the card. The slits should be about 2 inches (5 cm) apart and slightly longer than the width of the thermometer. See the diagram.
4. Insert the thermometer through the slits in the card.
5. Read and record the temperature on the thermometer. You may have to pull part of the thermometer out of the card in order to read the scale. Be sure not to touch the bulb end with your fingers, because the heat from your body will change the temperature reading.
6. Stand the dinosaur card outdoors so that the thermometer is in direct sunlight.
7. After 5 minutes, read and record the temperature.
8. Stand the dinosaur card in a shady area for 5 minutes, then read and record the temperature.

Results The temperature reading increases when the card is placed in direct sunlight and decreases when placed in the shade.

Why? Some dinosaurs, like reptiles of today, were **ectothermic** (having a body temperature that changes with the environment). They were able to regulate their body temperature by moving into and out of the sun. The higher temperature reading when the thermometer was placed in the sun indicates that the dinosaur's skin would have received more heat when the animal stood in a sunny area. The blood in the vessels beneath the skin would have warmed, raising the body temperature of the animal.

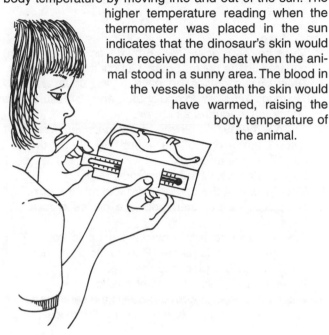

52. Cover-Up

Purpose To determine whether dinosaur eggs were laid in open nests.

Materials

masking tape
two 1-quart (1-liter) jars
1-cup (250-ml) measuring cup
tap water
marking pen
2 paper towels
2 rubber bands
cookie sheet
½ cup (125 ml) sand-leaf mixture (made by mixing equal parts of sand and leaves)

Procedure

1. Place a strip of tape down the side of each jar.
2. Pour 3 cups (750 ml) of water into each jar.
3. Use the pen to mark the level of the water on the tape.
4. Cover the top of each jar with a paper towel and secure with a rubber band.
5. Place the jars on the cookie sheet near a window with direct sunlight.
6. On the paper towel covering one of the jars, place a thick layer of the sand-leaf mixture.
7. Observe the water level in the jars every day for 2 weeks, or until one of the jars is empty.

Results The water level in the jar covered only with the paper towel is lower than the water level in the jar covered with the sand-leaf mixture.

Why? The shells of dinosaur eggs, like the paper towel, were porous. If the eggs had been exposed to air, their contents would have dried out. It is believed, therefore, that the eggs were covered with sand and plants. This covering not only kept the eggs from drying out, but also protected them from **predators** (animals that hunt and kill other animals for food) and kept them warm.

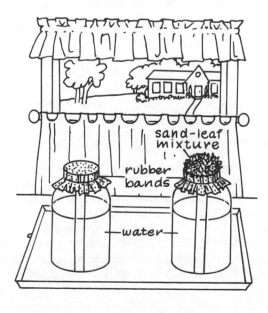

53. Dinosaur Puzzle

Purpose To represent the difficulty of identifying and assembling dinosaur bones.

Materials ruler
marking pen
white poster board
scissors
2 paper lunch bags
timer
writing paper
helper

Procedure

1. Measure and draw two 6-by-6-inch (15-by-15-cm) squares on the poster board. Cut out the two squares.
2. Draw puzzle pieces on each of the squares. Draw *Tyrannosaurus rex* on one square and *Parasaurolopus* on the other square, as shown.
3. Cut out the puzzle pieces of *Tyrannosaurus rex,* and place them in one of the paper bags. Label the bag "Tyrannosaurus rex."
4. Repeat step 3 for *Parasaurolopus.*
5. Choose one of the bags. Shake it to mix the puzzle pieces inside, then pour the pieces onto a table.
6. Ask a helper to time how long it takes you to arrange the puzzle pieces. Record the time, then return the puzzle pieces to the bag.
7. Repeat step 6, using the other puzzle.
8. Place the pieces of both puzzles in the same bag, and shake the bag to thoroughly mix the pieces.
9. Pour all the pieces onto the table, and as before, ask your helper to time how long it takes you to arrange both of the puzzles. Record the time.
10. Add the time needed to arrange the two puzzles individually and compare it to the time needed to arrange the mixed puzzles.

Results It usually takes longer to arrange the mixed puzzle pieces than to arrange the two puzzles individually.

Why? When the pieces of the two puzzles were mixed together, the pieces belonging to each puzzle had to be identified and separated before they could be arranged. This problem occurs when bones of different dinosaurs are found in the same area. Scientists must first identify the bones and then separate them before the bones can be assembled.

TYRANNOSAURUS REX

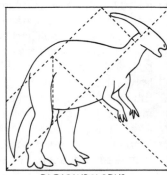

PARASAUROLOPUS

54. Hearing Without Ears

Purpose To demonstrate how a fish hears without external ears.

Materials new, unsharpened pencil
dishwashing liquid
tap water
paper towel
helper

Procedure

1. Wash the pencil with dishwashing liquid and water, and dry it on the paper towel.
2. Place the unsharpened end of the pencil between your teeth.
3. Cover your ears with your hands.
4. Ask your helper to rub the eraser end of the pencil with his or her finger. Make note of any sound heard.

Results A loud scratching sound is heard.

Why? **Sound** is a form of energy produced by **vibrations** (repeated back and forth motions) that travel through air or other materials. **Conduction** is the process by which types of energy, including sound, travel through a substance called a conductor. Rubbing the pencil causes it to vibrate. As the **molecules** (the smallest parts of a substance that have all the properties of the substance) in the pencil vibrate, they bump into neighboring molecules and start them vibrating. These vibrations travel up the pencil to your teeth, through the bones in your head, and on to your inner ear. Fish do not have outer ears as you do, but do have something like your inner ear: the labyrinth. Vibrations from the water move through the bones of the fish's head to the labyrinth. Your inner ear and the labyrinth of a fish report sounds to the brain, where hearing takes place.

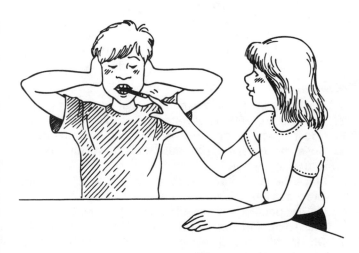

55. Bounce Back

Purpose To demonstrate how toothed whales "see" with their ears.

Materials small rectangular glass cooking pan
tap water
sheet of typing paper

Procedure
1. Fill the cooking pan about half full with water.
2. Place the pan on the paper.
3. With your finger, touch the surface of the water in the middle of one of the longer sides of the pan.
4. Observe the surface of the water.

Results Waves move back and forth across the surface of the water.

Why? Touching the water sends out **water waves** (a disturbance on the surface of water that repeats itself). These waves bounce off the solid sides of the pan and are reflected back toward their starting point. Like the water waves, sound waves will reflect off solid objects. The sound that is heard when sound waves bounce back from a surface is called an **echo**. Toothed whales, such as killer whales and sperm whales, are said to "see" with their ears because they send out sharp clicking sounds. These sounds reflect off objects such as fish and return to the whale. The time it takes for the sound to go out and come back is called the **echo time.** If the echo time is long, the whale knows the fish are far away. This process of finding the direction and distance of objects by the sounds reflected from them is called **echolocation.**

56. Pickup

Purpose To demonstrate how toothed whales hear echoes.

Materials 2 new, unsharpened pencils
3 feet (1 m) of size 10 crochet thread

Procedure
1. Tie one end of the thread to the center of each pencil.
2. Lay one of the pencils on the floor and stand on it with one foot.
3. Hold the thread taut by raising the other pencil.
4. Pluck the thread and listen to the sound.
5. Leaning forward so the thread doesn't touch your body, press the pencil against your jaw.
6. Now pluck the thread again and listen.

Result The sound is louder when the pencil is pressed against your jaw.

Why? At first the sound produced by the thread traveled through the air to your ears. When you pressed the pencil against your jaw, the sound traveled through the bones in your head to your ears. The loudness of a sound increases as the **density** (a measure of how much material of an object is packed into a given volume) of the material the sound travels through increases. Objects whose material are more **compact** (squeezed together) are said to be more **dense** than other objects because they contain more materials in the same volume. The solid bones in your jaw are much denser than air. Thus, the sound was louder when you held the pencil against your jaw. The toothed whale uses a similar method to hear sound underwater. It sends out clicking sounds, which bounce off solid objects. This echoed sound is picked up by the whale's jawbone and travels to its inner ear. Whales have outer ears, but the ears are not in a good position to hear sounds coming from in front of the whale.

57. Coated

Purpose To demonstrate the effect that oil spills can have on birds.

Materials 2 small bowls
tap water
3 tablespoons (45 ml) oil
two 2- to 3-inch (5- to 7.5-cm) -long feathers
(can be purchased at a crafts store)

NOTE: Do not pick up bird feathers from the ground outdoors. They can carry diseases.

Procedure
1. Fill the bowls three-fourths full with water.
2. Pour the oil into one of the bowls.
3. Gently lay one of the feathers on the surface of the water in the bowl without the oil.
4. Lift the feather from the bowl and blow on it.
5. Gently lay the second feather on the surface of the oil in the second bowl.
6. Lift the feather from the bowl and blow on it.

Results The feather taken from the water appears dry and is light enough to be moved by your breath. The feather taken from the oil appears wet and heavy. It moves little or not at all when you blow on it.

Why? Water does not stick to the feathers of birds very easily, but oil does. The oil-coated feather is very heavy,

and the fibers of the feather stick together. This experiment demonstrates how oil from oil spills can mat the feathers of birds and make the birds too heavy to fly. This makes the birds easy prey (animal hunted for food) to predators.

58. Too Much, Too Fast

Purpose To demonstrate the effect of overfishing.

Materials scissors
2 dishwashing sponges
ruler
large bowl of tap water
2 tea strainers—1 small, 1 large
small bowl
pencil
writing paper
helper

Procedure
1. Cut each sponge into 1-inch (2.5-cm) cubes.
2. Place 10 sponge cubes in the bowl of water, spreading the cubes over the water's surface.
3. Ask your helper to close his or her eyes and move the small strainer through the water once to scoop up as many cubes as possible.
4. Remove the cubes from the strainer and place them in the small bowl.
5. Count the cubes remaining in the water, and add an equal number of cubes to double the amount of cubes in the water.
6. Repeat steps 3 to 5 three times. On the last scooping, do not add any cubes. Record the number of cubes in the water.
7. Start over with 10 cubes in the water.
8. Ask your helper to do steps 3 and 4 four times, using the large strainer. Do not add cubes between scoopings. After the last time, count the cubes remaining in the water and add an equal number of cubes to double

the amount of cubes in the water. Record the number of cubes.

Results The number of cubes in the bowl of water increases when the small strainer is used and cubes are added after each scooping. The number of cubes greatly decreases and may even be zero after four scoops with the large strainer.

Why? The sponge cubes represent fish and the strainers commercial fishing nets. Scooping with the small strainer is like fishing with fewer nets and catching fewer fish. Adding cubes represents reproduction of fish. Commercial fishing boats haul in more fish. **Overfishing** removes fish faster than they can reproduce, as demonstrated by using the large strainer and not adding cubes after each scooping. Some fish are in danger of becoming extinct (no longer in existence) because of overfishing.

59. Slow Shuffle

Purpose To show how emperor penguins carry their eggs.

Materials 1 cup (250 ml) dry rice
sock

Procedure
1. Pour the rice into the sock.
2. Tie a knot in the sock.
3. Stand with your feet together.
4. Place the sock of rice on top of your feet.
5. Try to walk without dropping the sock off your feet.

Results The sock stays on your feet only if you move short distances at a time.

Why? Female emperor penguins lay 1 egg, which the male rolls on top of his feet. The egg stays in this position until it hatches, about 2 months later. To move around without dropping the egg, the penguin must do a slow shuffle like the shuffle you did with the sock of rice. But emperor penguins do have a little extra help from a flap of skin that folds down over the egg. This skin helps to keep the egg in place and also keeps it warm. Staying warm is difficult since emperor penguins hatch their eggs during the antarctic winter, where winds at times blow in excess of 100 miles per hour (160 kph), and the temperature can drop to −80°F (−62°C). After the egg hatches, the male and female take turns carrying their baby chick around on their feet for about another 2 months. This keeps the chick from freezing until its fat layer and protective feathers develop.

60. Paddles

Purpose To determine why penguins' wings are good for swimming.

Materials scissors
ruler
sheet of typing paper
large bowl of water

Procedure
1. Cut two 2-by-8-inch (5-by-20-cm) strips from the paper.
2. Holding one short end of one of the paper strips, try to push the water back and forth with the other end of the strip.
3. Fold the second paper strip in half from side to side. Fold it again from top to bottom.
4. Repeat step 2, using the folded paper.

Results The folded paper pushes the water back and forth, while the unfolded paper bends and doesn't push the water very well.

Why? The unfolded paper bends as it moves through the water, much like the wings of most birds. Thus, these wings are not useful for swimming. The folded paper easily pushes the water back and forth. Like the paper, the wings of a penguin are small and stiff, and act like paddles as they push the penguin through the water.

61. Divers

Purpose To determine how the density of a penguin's body affects its diving and swimming ability.

Materials 1-quart (1-liter) widemouthed jar
tap water
1-tablespoon (15-ml) measuring spoon
3 tablespoons (45 ml) table salt
2 film canisters with lids
masking tape
pen
ruler

Procedure
1. Fill the jar with water.
2. Pour 1 tablespoon (15 ml) of salt in one of the film canisters and close the lid.
3. Use the masking tape and pen to label the canister 1.
4. Add 2 tablespoons (30 ml) of salt to the other film canister, close its lid, and label it 2.
5. Place the canisters in the jar of water. Observe the level where each floats in the water.
6. Remove the canisters from the water, hold canister 1 about 2 inches (5 cm) above the water, then drop it.
7. Observe how far the canister sinks in the water.
8. Repeat steps 6 and 7, using canister 2.

Results When canister 1 is floating, it leans, and more of it is below the water than canister 2. When dropped into the water, canister 2 sinks to a deeper depth and takes longer to rise than does canister 1.

Why? The canisters are the same size, but canister 2 is heavier because the extra salt gives it more **mass** (the amount of material in an object). Thus, canister 2 has a greater density, or mass per volume, than canister 1. The greater the density of an object, the more easily it sinks in water. Penguins are heavier than most birds. This body weight is partly due to their solid, heavy bones. Unlike penguins, which don't fly, flying birds have light bones filled with lots of air. The penguins' heavier weight makes it easier for them to dive deeper. They also float lower in the water, which lets them use their powerful wings to push themselves along. Lighter birds that float high in the water can only use their feet to push themselves along when they swim.

62. Coiled

Purpose To model the movement of the feeding tube of butterflies and moths.

Materials party blower

Procedure
1. Place the party blower upside down in your mouth so that the end hangs down and coils toward your body.
2. Blow into the tube, then suck the air out.

Results The party blower uncoils, then coils again.

Why? The **proboscis** (feeding tube) of butterflies and moths stays coiled under the insect's head when not in use. To uncoil the tube, blood from the insect's body is forced into the proboscis, similar to the way you forced air into the party blower. When uncoiled, the proboscis is used by the insect to reach into flowers and suck up nectar (a sugary liquid).

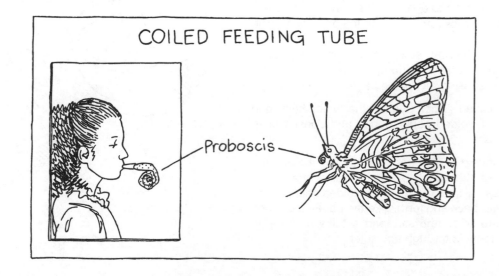

COILED FEEDING TUBE

Proboscis

63. Juicy

Purpose To model how flies eat.

Materials eyedropper
baby food jar of sweet potatoes
craft stick
masking tape
pen

Procedure

1. Place the tip of the eyedropper just below the surface of the potatoes in the jar. Try to fill the eyedropper with the sweet potatoes. Observe the amount of sweet potatoes that enter the eyedropper, if any.
2. Wash the eyedropper and allow it to dry.
3. Collect as much saliva in your mouth as possible, put the saliva on the craft stick, and transfer the saliva to the surface of the potatoes in the jar. Close the jar.
4. Using a pen and a piece of tape across the lid and down the sides of the jar, label the jar Do Not Eat.
5. Place the jar in the refrigerator and leave it undisturbed for 1 day.
6. After 24 hours, remove the jar from the refrigerator and repeat step 1.

Results On your first try, you can draw little or no potatoes into the eyedropper. After the saliva has been in the jar for 24 hours, the potatoes at the surface are liquid. You can then easily draw them into the eyedropper.

Why? Human **saliva** (liquid that softens and breaks down food), like the saliva of flies and many other insects, contains a chemical called **amylase**. Amylase breaks down **starch**, a complex chemical found in many foods, into less complex chemicals. In the experiment, the amylase in your saliva **digested** (broke down into an absorbable form) the potatoes, turning them to liquid. As you did in the experiment, flies drop saliva on the food they plan to eat. The amylase in the fly saliva quickly begins to digest the starch in the food. The spongy end of the fly's proboscis then soaks up the liquid and the insect sucks it in through the tube.

64. Singers

Purpose To model how crickets make sounds.

Materials index card
fingernail file or emery board

Procedure

1. Hold the index card upright so that one long edge rests on a table.
2. Support the card with one hand as you quickly draw the rough side of the file across the top edge of the card two times.
3. Wait 1 second and repeat steps 1 and 2.

Results You hear a rasping sound.

Why? When you rub the file across the paper, the rough surface of the file plucks the paper's edge, causing it to vibrate. The vibrating paper produces sound. Certain insects, like crickets and grasshoppers, produce sounds in much the same way. These insects make sounds by rubbing two body parts, usually one sharp-edged and the other rough or filelike, against each other. This process is called **stridulation.**

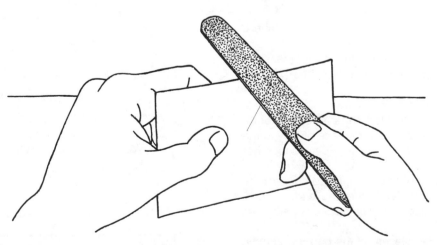

65. Clingers

Purpose To model how fleas hold on to their hosts.

Materials   scissors
ruler
10 feet (3 m) of rug yarn
masking tape
4-by-8-inch (10-by-20-cm) piece of cardboard
medium-tooth comb

Procedure

1. Cut a 6-inch (15-cm) piece from one end of the yarn and set it aside.
2. Spread the fingers of one hand apart and wrap the remaining yarn around your fingers.
3. Remove the loop of yarn from your hand.
4. Tie the strands together with the small, 6-inch (15-cm) piece of yarn.
5. Tape the ends of the small piece of yarn to the center of one short end of the cardboard.
6. Cut the bottom of the loop so that you have straight pieces of yarn.
7. Lay the cardboard on a table.
8. Holding the taped end of the yarn, push the teeth of the comb into the yarn. Try to comb the yarn.

Results The comb sticks in the yarn.

Why? The teeth of the comb are not spaced apart widely enough to easily pass through the yarn. A flea has spiny structures on its head similar to the teeth of the comb. The flea's spiny head sticks in the thick hair or fur of animals, the way the comb stuck in the yarn, keeping the flea from falling off the animal.

66. 3-D

Purpose To make a model of an adult insect's three main body parts.

Materials   4-ounce (113-g) stick of clay
sheet of paper
ruler
table knife
round toothpick
pencil
4-by-8-inch (10-by-20 cm) unruled index card

Procedure

1. Lay the clay on the paper. Roll the clay into a tube 6 inches (15 cm) long.
2. Use the knife to cut the clay roll into three pieces: 1 inch (2.5 cm), 2 inches (5 cm), and 3 inches (7.5 cm) long.
3. Round the ends of each piece of clay.
4. Break the toothpick in half. Use one half of the toothpick to connect the 1-inch (2.5-cm) piece of clay to the 2-inch (5-cm) piece. Push the two clay pieces together so they touch.
5. Use the remaining half of the toothpick to connect the 3-inch (7.5-cm) piece of clay to the free end of the 2-inch (5-cm) piece. Push the clay pieces together as before.
6. Lay the connected clay pieces on the paper and mold them into the shape of an insect's body as shown.

7. Place the clay model on the index card and label the parts as shown.

Results You have made a three-dimensional model of an insect's main body parts.

Why? An adult insect's body is divided into three main body parts: the head, the thorax, and the abdomen. The **head** is the front part, the **thorax** is the middle part, and the **abdomen** is the hind part. Every insect has the same three body parts.

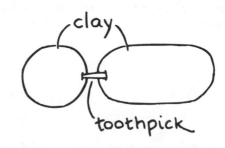

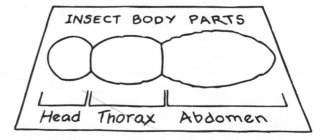

67. Boy or Girl?

Purpose To identify the gender (sex) of a cricket.

Materials sharpened pencil
1-quart (1-liter) resealable plastic bag
8 to 10 crickets (can be purchased at a pet store)
magnifying lens

Procedure
1. Prepare a temporary observing bag by using the point of the pencil to make 15 to 20 small airholes through both layers of the top of the bag.
2. Place one cricket in the bag.
3. Hold the cricket still by gently pressing the bag against its body. Use the magnifying lens to study the hind end of the cricket. Use the figures shown to determine if the cricket is a male or a female.
4. Within 5 minutes, remove the cricket from the observing bag.
5. Repeat steps 2 through 4 to identify the sex of each of the remaining crickets.

Results Some of the crickets are identified as male and some as female.

Why? You can tell male crickets from female crickets by looking at their abdomens. Every cricket has two feelers on its hind end, but the female has a third tube. It looks sort of like a stinger, but it's not. It's an egg-laying tube called an **ovipositor.**

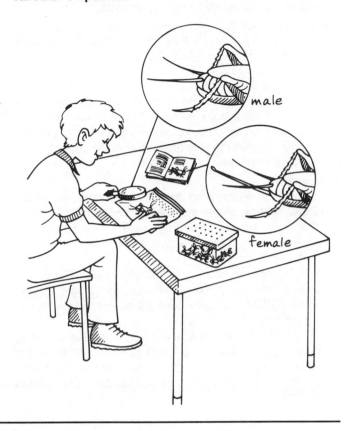

68. Lifters

Purpose To demonstrate how handling a butterfly affects its ability to fly.

Materials ruler
1-by-8-inch (2.5-by-20-cm) strip of typing paper
six ¾-inch (1.9-cm) round color-coding labels, 3 different colors
scissors

Procedure
1. About 2 inches (5 cm) from one short end of the paper strip, place a row of 2 labels of the same color side by side. The first label should go next to the long edge of the paper strip. The second label will stick out from the opposite edge.
2. Add 2 more rows of different colored labels across the paper. Start each row on the opposite edge of the paper, and overlap the labels in the previous row, as shown.
3. Cut off the parts of the labels that stick out from the edges of the paper. This strip will be your butterfly wing.
4. Hold the end near the labels against your chin, just below your bottom lip. Blow hard just above the top of the paper and observe the movement of the paper.
5. Bend up 1 or 2 of the labels near your mouth, then repeat step 4.

Results When you blow on the paper with the labels flat, the paper lifts, but the paper does not lift when the labels are bent up.

Why? The paper lifts when you blow over it because of the change in air pressure. (**Pressure** is the amount of force on an area.) The faster-moving air above the paper produces lower pressure than the slower-moving air below the paper. The paper moves from the area of high pressure to the area of low pressure. This upward force on the paper due to the flow of air over it is called **lift.** Insects that fly use lift. Butterflies and other flying insects, such as moths, have tiny colored scales on their wings. Touching a butterfly can remove or bend the scales. This can make it hard for the insect to fly, the same way that bending the labels makes it hard for the paper to lift.

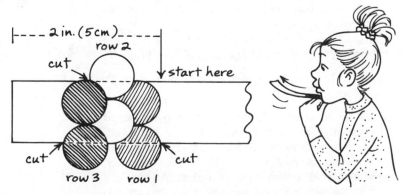

69. Water Walkers

Purpose To model water-walking insects.

Materials scissors
1-by-3-inch (2.5-by-7.5-cm) strip of corrugated cardboard (from a box)
pen
ruler
12-inch (30-cm) cotton terry stem (special pipe cleaners available at craft stores), or use a chenille craft stem (available at craft stores)
petroleum jelly (if using chenille craft stem)
large bowl of tap water

Procedure

1. Cut the cardboard strip into an insect shape as shown. Draw eyes on one end of the strip.
2. Cut three 4-inch (10-cm) pieces from the cotton terry stem. If using a chenille craft stem, coat the sections with petroleum jelly.
3. Stick the pieces of stem all the way through three cardboard grooves in the middle section of the insect's body so that the same amount of stem sticks out on either side.
4. Bend each leg down where it meets the insect's body. Then, bend out about 1/4 inch (0.63 cm) of the end of each leg to form a foot. Stand the insect on a table and adjust the bends in the legs so that each foot touches the table.

5. Slowly lower the insect into the water until its feet touch the surface of the water, then release it.

Results The insect stands on the water's surface.

Why? The molecules of water cling together at the surface to form a skinlike film. The attractive force that causes this is called **surface tension.** Because water has surface tension, some lightweight bugs can walk across the surface without sinking. At first, the terry stems in this experiment, like the hair covering the bodies of some water bugs, do not get wet. Unlike the hairs on a water insect, the terry stems in time do become wet and the model insect sinks.

70. Bug-Eyed

Purpose To model an insect's eye.

Materials scissors
cardboard tube from toilet tissue
24 drinking straws
transparent tape

Procedure

1. Cut a slit down the tube so that it opens.
2. Stand the straws together on a flat surface and wrap the tube around the straws. Secure the tube with tape.
3. Hold the free end of the tube near, but not touching, your eye.
4. Close one eye and look through the tube with your open eye. Look at a moving object, such as the rotating blades of a fan.
5. As you continue to look through the tube, slowly move it to arm's length away from your body.

Results Tiny separate images are seen through the straws.

Why? Most insects have two large eyes called **compound eyes,** one on each side of the head. These eyes are made up of thousands of separate units called **ommatidia.** At the surface of each ommatidium is a lens called a **facet.** (A **lens** is a part of the eye that focuses light rays.) The omma-

tidia are grouped together so that the facets form a honeycomb pattern. Each ommatidium receives a small amount of light from the total scene that the insect sees. These separate images are sent to the brain, where they are combined to form the whole picture. Scientists don't know what an insect actually sees. This experiment gives you an idea of what it might be like to receive images from the multiple facets of a compound eye.

71. Fly Away

Purpose To model how some young spiders move to a new area.

Materials scissors
ruler
spool of sewing thread
six ¾-inch (1.9-cm) round
   color-coding labels

Procedure

1. Cut 6 pieces of thread, each about 6 inches (15 cm) long.
2. Attach one end of a thread to one of the labels by folding the label, sticky sides together, over the end of the thread. You have made a model of a spiderling.
3. Repeat step 2 five times to make 5 more spiderlings.
4. Lay the spiderlings together on a table.
5. Bend down toward the table so that your mouth is close to, but not touching, the spiderlings. Then, blow as hard as you can.

Results The spiderlings fly away.

Why? Some young spiders, or **spiderlings,** climb onto branches or other objects and release silk. As the silk lines lengthen, any wind lifts the small spider off its perch and it floats on the wind to a new area. This technique spider-

lings use to float through the air and move to new areas is called **ballooning.** The flying models in this experiment represent ballooning spiderlings.

72. Covered

Purpose To collect a spiderweb.

Materials scissors
black construction paper
small round plastic container, such as an empty, clean cottage cheese or margarine container
orb web (spiral shaped)
scissors
adult helper

NOTE: Use a spider field guide to identify an orb web. These webs are often found between tree branches or porch pillars. Make sure the spider isn't in the web before doing the experiment.

Procedure

1. Cut a circle from the construction paper to fit in the bottom of the plastic container and place it in the container.
2. Place the mouth of the container against the spiderweb.
3. Push the container forward to break off the part of the web covering the mouth of the container. Ask your helper to use the scissors to cut the web strands so that the web is stretched across the mouth of the container.

NOTE: Keep the web for the next experiment.

Results A spiderweb is collected.

Why? Orb weavers are spiders that build beautiful spiral-like webs. These webs are woven in open areas, often between objects, such as tree branches or flower stems. Strands of silk are released from the spider's silk gland, and its **spinnerets** (silk-spinning organs) are used to form silk lines that radiate out from the center of the web like spokes of a wheel. Coiling silk lines connect the spokes. This web traps flying insects or any insect that might wander into the web. Follow the procedure in the next experiment to study the parts of the web.

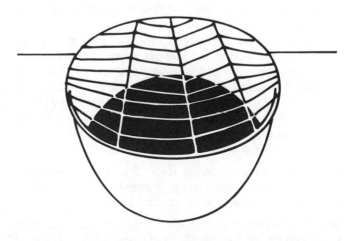

73. Snares

Purpose To study the strands of an orb web.

Materials orb web from Experiment 72, "Covered"
desk lamp
magnifying lens
pencil

Procedure
1. Place the web under the desk lamp.
2. Use the magnifying lens to study the strands of the web. Note the differences in the strands.
3. Gently press the eraser end of the pencil against one of the strands in the web and lift up. Does the web stick to the eraser?
4. Try step 3 again on a different-looking strand.

Results Some of the strands are smooth and some look like a beaded necklace. The beaded strands stick to the pencil eraser.

Why? The strands of silk in a spiderweb are different. Some spider silk dries when air touches it and some silk stays sticky. The sticky beaded strands are made from a combination of dry and sticky silk. Silk flows out of tiny holes in the spider's spinnerets. The spinnerets move in fingerlike motion as they coat a dry silk strand with sticky silk. The spider then uses the claws on its legs to puck the strand. The plucking causes the liquid silk to separate into

tiny beads along the strand. The sticky strands hold on to any insects that fly or walk into the web until the spider can come and get them. The spider can walk along the dry strands and not get stuck. It also has oil on its feet that prevents it from getting stuck on the sticky strands.

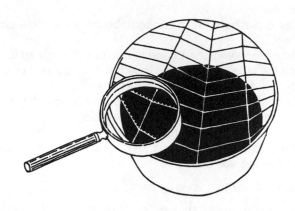

74. Slow Thinking

Purpose To trick your brain.

Materials 5 crayons or markers—red, blue, green, black, and orange
2 sheets of typing paper
timer
helper

Procedure
1. Use each crayon to write the name of another color in a column on the paper as shown. For example, use the green crayon to write Red, the black crayon to write Green, and so on.
2. Ask your helper to time you. When your helper says go, look at the words, but instead of reading the words, identify the color of the letters and say the color out loud. For example, Black is written with a red crayon, so when you look at the printed word Black, say red.
3. Repeat steps 1 and 2, writing the names of animals, such as Bird, Frog, Dog, Fish, and Cat, using a different color for each word.

Results It takes longer to name the color of a written word if the letters spell out a different color than if they spell out other objects such as animals.

Why? Scientists think that the human brain has one storage place for the names of objects, and another place for

the names of colors. When you look at the word Red printed in green, your brain tries to search both of the storage places at once and finds two different answers, which results in a conflict in what to respond. It is much easier and faster to name the colors if the words describe other objects, such as bird, frog, and so on, instead of colors.

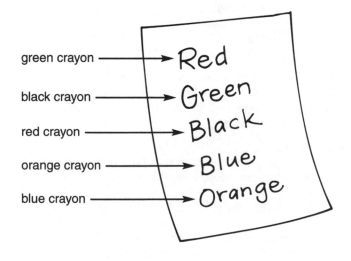

green crayon → Red
black crayon → Green
red crayon → Black
orange crayon → Blue
blue crayon → Orange

75. Smelly

Purpose To determine how temperature affects odor.

Materials 4 tablespoons (120 ml) chocolate ice cream
two 5-ounce (150-ml) paper cups

Procedure

1. Place 2 tablespoons (60 ml) of ice cream in each cup.
2. Place one cup in the freezer and leave the other cup sitting at room temperature.
3. Allow the cups to sit undisturbed overnight.
4. Remove the cup from the freezer and smell its contents.
5. Smell the contents of the unchilled cup and compare it to the smell of the other cup's contents.

Results The unchilled ice cream has a stronger chocolate smell.

Why? **Odor** is the property of a substance that activates the sense of smell. Materials give off odor when they **vaporize,** which means they change to a **vapor** (gas). When a vapor enters your nose, it is picked up by smell detectors, which send a message to your brain. The more vapor that enters the nose at one time, the stronger the smell. The warmer the material, the more it vaporizes and the more its odor gets into your nose. Very cold materials vaporize so little that they have little or no odor.

76. Cell Model

Purpose To construct a model that shows three parts of a cell.

Materials lemon gelatin dessert mix
1-pint (125-ml) resealable plastic bag
1-quart (1-liter) bowl
large grape
adult helper

Procedure

1. Have your adult helper mix the ingredients for the gelatin dessert according to the instructions on the box.
2. Allow the gelatin to cool to room temperature.
3. Pour the gelatin into the resealable bag, seal the bag, and place it in the bowl.
4. Set the bowl and bag in the refrigerator and chill until the gelatin is firm (about 3 to 4 hours).
5. Remove the gelatin from the refrigerator and open the bag.
6. Using your finger, insert the grape into the center of the gelatin.
7. Reseal the bag.

Results A model of a cell with three parts is made.

Why? All the **cells** (smallest unit of all living things) in your body, like the model, have these three parts: a cell membrane, cytoplasm, and a nucleus. The plastic bag, like

a **cell membrane,** keeps the parts of the cell together and acts as a barrier to protect the inner parts. The pale color of the gelatin dessert simulates the grayish jellylike material, called **cytoplasm,** that fills the cell. It is in the cytoplasm that most of the chemical work of the cell takes place. Floating in the gelatin is a grape that represents the **nucleus,** the cell's governing body. The cell membrane, cytoplasm, and nucleus all work together and are necessary for the life of the cell.

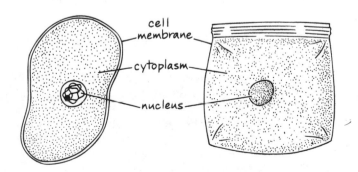

77. Lub-Dub

Purpose   To listen to sounds produced by the heart.

Materials   cardboard tube from paper towel roll
helper

Procedure

1. In a quiet room, ask your helper to sit in a chair and hold the paper tube against his or her chest. The tube should be slightly to the left side of the chest.
2. Place one of your ears over the other end of the tube.
3. Stand very still and listen to the sound of your helper's heart.

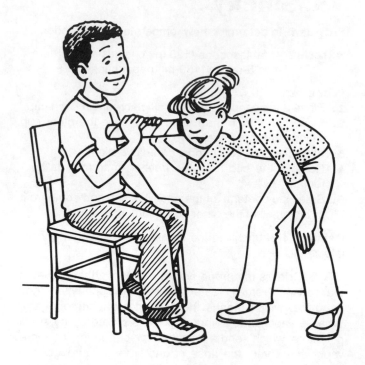

Results   Your helper's heart makes a "lub-*dub*" sound.

Why?   A **stethoscope** is a medical instrument used to listen to sounds within the body, specifically those made by the heart and lungs. The paper tube works much like the hollow tube stethoscope invented in 1819 by R. T. H. Laennec (1781–1826), a French physician. Heart sounds are the sounds made by the heart's **valves** (flaps of tissue that control the flow of blood or other liquids in the body) as they shut. The softer "lub" sound is heard when the valves shut in the top chambers of the heart. The louder *"dub"* sound is heard when the heart valves shut the big vessels leaving the heart.

78. Heartbeat

Purpose   To measure your heart rate.

Materials   watch with second hand

Procedure

1. Lay your arm on a table with the palm of your hand up.
2. Place the fingertips of your other hand below the thumb on your upturned wrist.
3. Gently press until you can feel your heartbeat.
NOTE: You may have to move your fingertips around the area until you feel your heartbeat.
4. Count the number of heartbeats that you feel in 1 minute.

Results   A steady beating is felt by the fingertips. The number of beats will vary.

Why?   The number of times your heart beats in 1 minute is called your **heart rate.** Adults have an average heart rate of about 70 beats per minute when sitting quietly. Children usually have a faster rate of about 95 beats per minute. The rate for both children and adults increases with activity because your cells need more oxygen and food when you are more active.

79. Squeezed

Purpose To demonstrate how hard your heart works.

Materials   tennis ball
watch with second hand
paper
pencil
helper

Procedure
1. Hold the tennis ball in one hand.
2. Ask your helper to be the timekeeper. When your helper says start, squeeze the ball as many times as possible, counting each squeeze. When your helper says stop, at the end of 15 seconds, record the number of squeezes. How does your hand feel?
3. Multiply by 4 the number of squeezes in step 2 to determine the number of squeezes that would be made if you kept up the same pace for 60 seconds, or 1 minute. For example, if you made 40 squeezes in 15 seconds, then: 4 × 40 = 160 squeezes in 60 seconds.

Results The number of squeezes will vary, but squeezing the ball will make your hand feel tired.

Why? Each time your heart beats, it squeezes about as hard as your hand did in squeezing the tennis ball. At rest,

an adult's heart squeezes about 70 times and a child's squeezes about 95 times in 1 minute. Physical exercise causes the heart to work even harder and squeeze even more times in 1 minute.

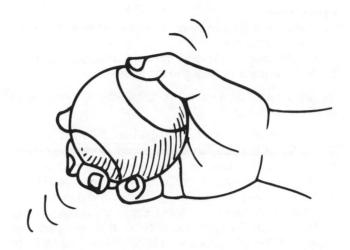

80. Uphill

Purpose To show the effect of gravity on blood flow.

Materials clock with second hand

Procedure
1. Stand against a wall with your left arm held high and your right arm down next to your right side.
2. At the end of 1 minute, put your hands together palms up.
3. Compare the color of your hands.

Results The right hand is darker than the left hand.

Why? Gravity pulls everything down, including the blood in your body. The pumping of your heart keeps all the blood from settling at your lowest point, but the heart can't totally compete with gravity. When you hold the left hand up and the right hand down, more blood flows down into the right hand than gets pumped up into the left hand, so the right hand is darker.

81. Carriers

Purpose   To identify veins and capillaries.

Materials   flashlight
hand mirror

Procedure

1. Raise your tongue and shine the light on the area under the tongue.
2. Use the mirror to inspect the area under your tongue.
3. Find the parts identified in the figure.

Results   Large blue vessels and hair-thin red and bluish red vessels are seen.

Why?   Blood is carried through the body by blood vessels. The color of oxygen-rich blood is red, and oxygen-poor blood is blue or bluish red. The large blue blood vessels that carry oxygen-poor blood to the heart are called **veins.** The hair-thin red and bluish red blood vessels are called **capillaries.** Capillaries connect the ends of veins to the ends of arteries. Capillaries connected to veins contain bluish red, oxygen-poor blood. Capillaries connected to **arteries** (blood vessels that carry oxygen-rich blood from the heart) contain red oxygen-rich blood. Arteries are not easily seen under the tongue.

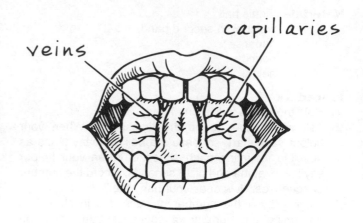

82. Upside Down

Purpose   To show how you swallow food.

Materials   chair without arms
cookie

Procedure

1. Lie across the chair.
2. Take a bite of the cookie, then chew and swallow it. Observe how chewing changes the cookie.

Results   The cookie piece is broken, turned to mush, and swallowed.

Why?   When you eat, food is chopped and ground by the teeth and mixed with saliva, which softens and partially digests the food. Your tongue rolls the mixture into a ball. This ball, called a **bolus,** is pushed into the food tube called the **esophagus.** The esophagus leads from the back of the throat to the **stomach,** a pouch where the bolus is further digested. As demonstrated by this experiment, you can swallow lying on your stomach because food doesn't just fall down your throat into your stomach. The contraction (squeezing together) of muscles inside the esophagus moves the bolus forward. This process is called **peristalsis.** You could even swallow upside down, but it isn't safe to do this because you might choke.

III
Chemistry

white Vinegar

blue litmus

red litmus

Cold

Warm

effervescent antacid tablets

83. On Line

Purpose   To compare SI and English volume units.

Materials   drinking glass
tap water
1-cup (250-ml) measuring cup

Procedure

1. Fill the glass with water.
2. Place the cup on a table or other flat surface. Sit or kneel at the table so that you view the 1-cup mark at eye level.
3. Slowly pour water from the glass into the cup until the water's surface reaches the 1-cup mark.
4. Turn the cup around and view the 250-ml mark on the cup. Is the water's surface above, at, or below this mark?

Results   The water's surface is level with the 1-cup mark, but below the 250-ml mark.

Why?   **Volume** is the amount of space something occupies. The English system has many units of liquid volume, including the **cup** used in this experiment. The **SI** (International System of Units) unit for liquid volume is the **liter.** (SI is commonly called the metric system of measurements.) The English cup is divided into fractions, such as ¼ cup or ½ cup, or into ounces. There are 8 ounces in 1 cup. The SI liter is based on multiples of 10. The liter is most often

divided into parts called milliliters (as in this experiment). There are 1,000 milliliters (ml) in 1 liter. Note that 1 cup is almost equal to 250 ml.

84. Full

Purpose   To measure the volume of a box.

Materials
pen	school glue
ruler	baking pan
30-by-30-cm piece of white poster board	500-ml measuring cup
marker	tap water

Procedure

1. Use the pen and ruler to divide the poster board into 1-cm squares.
2. With the marker and ruler, make darker solid and dashed lines as shown. Label the tabs and sides as shown.
3. Turn the paper over and fold the paper along one of the darker lines. Unfold the paper and repeat, folding along each darker line.
4. Cut along the dashed lines.
5. Fold sides A and D toward the center, then glue tab A to the back of side A. Be sure to cover the seams with glue.
6. Fold side B toward the center, then glue tab B to the back of side B. Continue folding and gluing until a box is formed.
7. Allow the glue to dry. Then set the box in the baking pan.
8. Fill the cup to the 500-ml mark with water. Slowly pour the water into the box.
9. Repeat step 8.

Results   One thousand milliliters of water fills the box.

Why?   The volume of a box is measured by multiplying its length by its width by its height. The box is 10 cm on each side, so its volume is 1,000 cubic cm, or cm^3 (10 cm × 10 cm × 10 cm). Volume is also measured in liters or portions of liters. One ml is the same volume as 1 cm^3. This means that 1,000 cm^3 is the same as 1,000 ml. Since 1,000 ml equals 1 liter, the box can be said to have a volume of 1 liter.

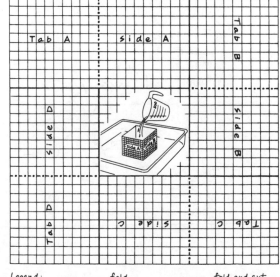

Legend: ———— fold   —·—·—·— fold and cut

85. Meltdown

Purpose To measure the volume of melted snow.

Materials 10-ounce (300-ml) transparent plastic drinking
glass
snow (Shaved or finely crushed ice will work if
snow is not available.)

Procedure

1. Scrape the glass across the snow to fill the glass. Take
care not to pack the snow in the glass. Fresh snow
works best.
2. Allow the filled glass to sit at room temperature until
the snow melts.
3. Note the amount of water in the glass.

Results When the snow melts, there is less than a full
glass of water.

Why? Snow is soft, white ice **crystals** (solid materials
whose atoms or molecules are arranged in a repeating
pattern). These crystals form when water vapor in the air
freezes. The process by which a vapor changes directly
into a solid without becoming a liquid is called **sublimation.** As the snow crystals fall through the **atmosphere**
(the blanket of gases surrounding a celestial body), they
cluster together and form snowflakes. A lot of air also
mixes with the snowflakes as the flakes fall to the ground.
The more air that is mixed with the snowflakes, the greater

the volume of the snow. When the snow melts, the air in
the mixture is released. The volume of snow is greater
than the volume of liquid water it becomes when melted.
Shaved or crushed ice is also a mixture of small ice crystals
and air. Like the snow, shaved ice has a greater volume
than the water it becomes when melted. But generally,
snow has more air mixed with it than does shaved or
crushed ice. Fresh snow has more air than older snow that
has had time to be more **compressed** (squeezed
together) by the weight of the snow above it.

86. Weighty

Purpose To determine the weight of water.

Materials food scale
2-cup (500-ml) measuring cup
pencil
writing paper
tap water

Procedure

1. Weigh the empty cup. Record the weight of the cup in
pounds (grams).
2. Fill the cup to the 2-cup (500-ml) mark with water and
weigh the filled cup.
3. Using the following example, fill in the missing measurements to calculate the weight of the water. (In the
English system, the weight will be in pounds and the
volume in cups. In the SI system, use grams and milliliters.)

weight of cup + water	=	? pounds (g)
− weight of cup	=	? pounds (g)
weight of 2 cups (500 ml) of water	=	? pounds (g)

Results The weight of 2 cups (500 ml) of water is determined.

Why? Weight is a measure of the gravitational force
pulling an object downward toward Earth's center. The
weight of 2 cups (500 ml) of water is about 1 pound. Two
cups is equal to 1 pint, thus the saying "A pint's a pound
the world around." This saying will help you remember
the weight of water. (In the SI system, 1 ml of water weighs
1 g.)

87. Size Matters

Purpose To prepare models of objects with similar mass but different density.

Materials   1-quart (1-liter) widemouthed jar
tap water
2 identical glass marbles
2 identical 7-inch (17.5-cm) round balloons

Procedure

1. Fill the jar three-fourths full with water.
2. Place a marble inside each balloon.
3. In one of the balloons, tie a knot as close to the marble as possible.
4. Slightly inflate the second balloon with air, and tie a knot as close to the mouth of the balloon as possible.
5. Drop both balloons in the jar of water. Observe what happens to the balloons.

Results The inflated balloon floats on the surface of the water, but the deflated balloon sinks to the bottom of the jar.

Why? Density is the measure of how much mass is packed into a given volume. Density is calculated by dividing an object's mass by its volume. The amount of air in either balloon has little mass, so the mass of each balloon is about the same. However, the inflated balloon has a greater volume. Since its volume is greater, its density is less. Objects that have a density less than water, such as the inflated balloon, will float in water.

88. Floater

Purpose To demonstrate a method of comparing the density of materials of equal volume.

Materials   cooking pot or bucket 8 inches (20 cm) deep or deeper
tap water
ruler
can of regular soda
can of diet soda (must be the same brand and flavor as regular soda)

Procedure

1. Fill the pot with water to a depth of 6 inches (15 cm).
2. Place the cans of soda in the water.
3. Observe the positions of the cans in the water.

Results The diet soda floats in the water, but the regular soda does not float.

Why? The diet soda floats, so the density of the diet soda must be less than that of the regular soda. Since the volume of the two sodas is the same, the mass of the diet soda must be less than that of the regular soda.

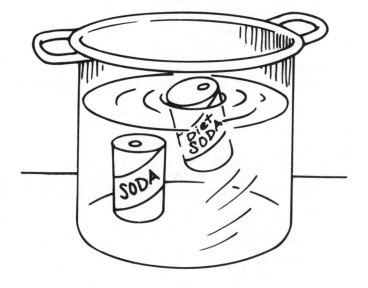

89. Compact

Purpose To demonstrate the effect that cold temperature has on the density of air.

Materials 9-inch (22-cm) round balloon
tape measure
marker
timer
helper

NOTE: This experiment requires a freezer.

Procedure

1. Inflate the balloon and tie a knot in it.
2. Use the tape measure to measure the **circumference** (the distance around a circle) of the largest part of the balloon. While the tape measure is wrapped around the balloon, ask a helper to use the marker to draw a line on the balloon along the edge of the tape to mark the circumference.
3. Place the balloon in the freezer. After 10 minutes, remove the balloon and again use the tape measure to measure the circumference of the balloon along the line drawn. Note any change in the size of the balloon.

Results The balloon's circumference is less when cooled.

Why? Cooling the balloon cools the air inside it. As the air cools, the air molecules slow down and move closer together. The air molecules do not push with as much force on the inside surface of the balloon, therefore the size of the balloon decreases. Since in the cooled balloon the same number of air molecules are taking up a smaller space, cold air is denser than the same number of molecules of warm air.

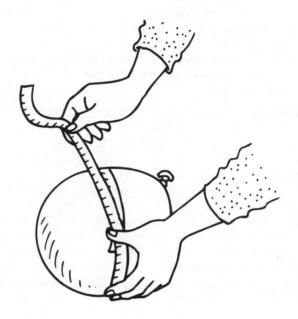

90. Sinkers

Purpose To demonstrate how the density of different liquids varies.

Materials masking tape
clear drinking glass
marking pen
ruler
cooking oil
1-cup (250-ml) measuring cup
water
light corn syrup

Procedure

1. Place a piece of tape down the side of the glass.
2. Using a marking pen and a ruler, mark three lines on the tape at these distances from the bottom of the glass: 1 inch (2.5 cm), 2 inches (5 cm), and 3 inches (7.5 cm).
3. Pour cooking oil into the glass up to the 1-inch (2.5-cm) mark on the tape.
4. Fill the measuring cup with water and slowly pour the water down the inside of the glass until the level of the liquid is at the 2-inch (5-cm) mark.
5. Observe the positions of the water and the oil in the glass.
6. Pour enough corn syrup into the glass to bring the surface of the liquid level with the 3-inch (7.5-cm) mark.
7. Observe the positions of all three liquids in the glass.

Results The three liquids form three separate layers. The syrup is on the bottom, the water is in the middle, and the oil floats on top.

Why? The liquids in this experiment separate according to their densities. Syrup is the most dense, so it sinks to the bottom. Oil is the least dense, so it floats on the top.

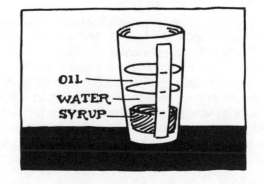

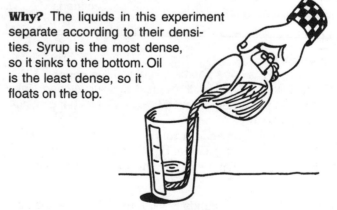

OIL
WATER
SYRUP

91. Riser

Purpose   To construct a hydrometer.

Materials   drinking glass
tap water
scissors
ruler
drinking straw
marking pen
grape-size piece of clay
3 BBs
1-teaspoon (5-ml) measuring spoon
5 teaspoons (25 ml) table salt
spoon

Procedure

1. Fill the glass about three-fourths full with water.
2. Cut a 4-inch (10-cm) section from the straw.
3. With the marking pen, draw lines dividing the straw equally into ten sections.
4. Plug one end of the straw piece with clay, then drop the BBs into the straw. You have made a hydrometer.
5. Stand the hydrometer, clay plug down, in the glass of water. Use the lines on the straw to determine the height of the hydrometer above the water's surface.
6. Remove the hydrometer from the water and add 1 teaspoon (5 ml) of salt to the water. Stir the water, then place the hydrometer back in the liquid. Again deter-

mine the height of the hydrometer above the water's surface.

7. Repeat step 4 four times, adding 1 teaspoon (5 ml) of salt each time until all of the salt has been added.

Results   With each addition of salt, the hydrometer rises higher in the water.

Why?   A **hydrometer** is an instrument used to measure the density of a liquid. This instrument rises or sinks in a liquid depending on the density of the liquid. The greater the density, the higher the hydrometer floats in the liquid. Adding salt to the water increased its density, so the hydrometer floated higher in the salty water.

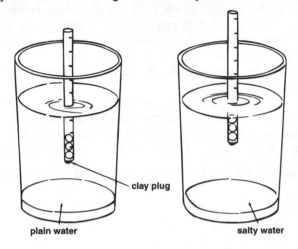

clay plug

plain water   salty water

92. Spraying Water

Purpose   To show that atoms have positive and negative parts.

Materials   9-inch (22.5-cm) round balloon

Procedure

1. Inflate the balloon and tie a knot in it.
2. Place the pot under the faucet in your kitchen sink. Turn on the water so that it falls in a small but continuous stream.
3. Rub the balloon against your hair, about five strokes. It is important that your hair be clean, dry, and oil free.
4. Hold the balloon near but not touching the running water.

Results   The water bends toward the balloon, and small streams of water spray out.

Why?   Water is an example of **matter** (any substance that has mass and takes up space). The smallest building blocks of matter are called **atoms.** An atom's center, called a **nucleus,** contains positively charged particles called **protons** and neutrally charged particles called **neutrons.** Spinning outside the positively charged nucleus are negatively charged particles called **electrons.** The balloon rubs the electrons off the hair and onto the balloon, giving the balloon an excess of negative charges. This buildup of charges is called **static electricity.** The positive charges

of the water are attracted to the negative charge of the balloon. This attraction between the positive and negative charges is great enough to pull the water toward the balloon.

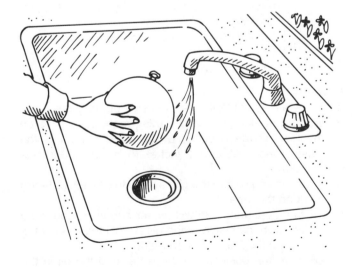

93. Phases

Purpose To observe the properties of the phases of matter.

Materials marker
three 3-ounce (90-ml) paper cups
tap water
3 cereal bowls

Procedure

1. Use the marker to label one of the cups Liquid and one of the cups Solid. Fill these cups about one-fourth full with water.
2. Place the cup labeled Solid in the freezer. Remove the cup from the freezer after the water has frozen (in 3 to 4 hours or so).
3. Label the remaining cup Gas. This cup is filled with air.
4.. Place all three cups together on a table. Observe the contents of each cup.
5. One at a time, pour the contents of each cup into a separate bowl. Observe the contents of each bowl.

Results The ice stays the same shape when poured into the bowl, but the water spreads out. The air is not visible.

Why? Solid, liquid, and gas are the three common forms of matter, called **phases of matter. Solids** have a definite shape and volume. The ice was the same shape and volume in the bowl as in the cup. **Liquids** have no definite shape but have a definite volume. The liquid water spread out in the bowl, but the amount of water was the same in the bowl as in the cup. **Gases,** such as air, have no definite shape or volume. The air moved in and out of the cup and bowl and spread around the room.

94. Slime

Purpose To produce a non-Newtonian fluid.

Materials spoon
1 teaspoon (5 ml) liquid starch
1 teaspoon (5 ml) white school glue
food coloring
12-inch (30-cm) square sheet of waxed paper
timer

Procedure

1. Using the spoon, mix the starch, glue, and 1 drop of food coloring in the center of the waxed paper. Continue to stir the materials until a substance forms that begins to separate from the paper.
2. Allow the substance to stand on the paper for 3 to 4 minutes. Then, with your fingers, roll the substance into a ball and knead it with your hands for about 1 minute. You have made slime.
3. Try these experiments, observing what happens to the slime each time.
   • Roll the slime into a ball and bounce it on a smooth surface.
   • Hold it in your hands and *quickly* pull the ends in opposite directions.
   • Hold it in your hands and *slowly* pull the ends in opposite directions.

NOTE: Keep the slime for Experiment 96, "Hot Stuff."

Results You have made a soft, pliable material that bounces slightly when dropped, breaks apart if pulled quickly, and stretches if pulled slowly.

Why? A **fluid** is a substance, such as a liquid or a gas, that can flow. A **non-Newtonian fluid** is a weird substance that has properties of both solids and liquids. This type of fluid acts like a solid and breaks when pressure is quickly applied. When left alone, it acts like a liquid and slowly flows to take the shape of whatever container it's put into. The slower the flow the higher is its **viscosity** (measure of how fast a fluid flows).

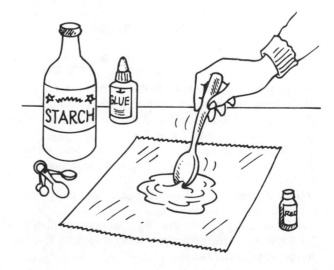

95. Springy

Purpose To demonstrate the cohesive force of water.

Materials cereal bowl
tap water
½-by-6-inch (1.25-by-15-cm) strip of office
paper

Procedure

1. Fill the bowl with water and set the bowl on a table.
2. Fold the paper strip forward and backward like an accordion. Space the folds about ½ inch (1.25 cm) apart.
3. Dip one end of the folded paper strip in the water and take it out again.
4. Holding the dry end of the folded strip, very slowly bring the wet end close to the surface of the water.
5. Observe what happens to the paper when it is just above the water's surface.

Results The paper springs toward the water.

Why? Water molecules have a positive and a negative side. The positive side of one molecule attracts the negative side of another. In this experiment, the water molecules on the paper are attracted to the water molecules on the surface of the water. The attraction between like molecules, such as water to water, is called a **cohesive force.** When the water molecules on the paper move toward the

water in the bowl, they pull the paper they are touching with them. The force that keeps the water attached to the paper is called an **adhesive force,** which means an attraction between unlike molecules.

96. Hot Stuff

Purpose To determine how an increase in temperature affects the cohesive force in a non-Newtonian fluid.

Material slime from Experiment 94, "Slime"
2 small cereal bowls
microwave oven
oven mittens
2 forks
timer
adult helper

Procedure

1. Divide the slime into 2 equal pieces, placing a piece in each bowl.
2. Place one bowl of slime on a table at room temperature.
3. Ask your adult helper to heat the second bowl of slime in a microwave for only 5 seconds. Ask the adult to use the oven mittens to remove the bowl from the microwave and place it on a table.
4. Use separate forks to stir and lift the slime in each bowl. Compare the samples' thickness and their ability to flow.
CAUTION: Do not allow the heated slime or bowl to touch your skin. It could burn your skin.
5. Continue to stir and lift the slime samples periodically for 5 minutes. This allows the heated sample to return to room temperature.

NOTE: Keep the bowls of slime for the next experiment.

Results The heated slime was thinner and flowed from the fork more quickly than the sample at room temperature. As the heated slime cooled, it returned to its original thickness and appeared to flow in a similar manner to the unheated slime.

Why? Heating a substance causes its molecules to vibrate more rapidly. This motion can overcome the cohesive force binding them together, allowing them to move around more freely. The heated slime was less **viscous** (thick), so it flowed more freely. As the slime cooled, the molecules vibrated less and cohesive force between the molecules again bound them tighter together. Thus, the unheated slime was more viscous and flowed more slowly. The slime is a non-Newtonian fluid, with both solid and liquid properties. When heated, the slime had fewer non-Newtonian properties and more liquid properties. But when the heated slime cooled, it again had the same non-Newtonian properties as it did before being heated.

97. Cold Stuff

Purpose To determine how a decrease in temperature affects the cohesive force in a non-Newtonian fluid.

Materials bowls of slime from Experiment 96, "Hot Stuff"
freezer
timer

Procedure

1. Set one bowl of slime on a table at room temperature and put the other bowl in a freezer.
2. Remove the slime from the freezer after it is frozen solid. This will take about 1 hour.
3. Using your fingers, pick up each piece of slime by one edge and compare the samples' thickness and ability to flow.
4. Repeat step 3 periodically until the frozen slime has warmed to room temperature. This my take 10 minutes or more.

Results The frozen slime was solid and did not flow as did the thinner slime at room temperature. As the frozen slime warmed, its ability to flow increased, and at room temperature, the flow of both samples appeared to be the same.

Why? Cooling a substance causes its molecules to vibrate more slowly and the cohesive force between the molecules to hold the molecules more tightly together. As the slime warmed, molecules vibrated faster. So, its cohesive force decreased, thus the molecules were less tightly held together, making the slime less viscous, and more able to flow. The slime is a non-Newtonian fluid, with properties of both solids and liquids. When cooled, the slime had fewer non-Newtonian properties and more solid properties. But when the cooled slime warmed to room temperature, it again had the same non-Newtonian properties as it did before being cooled.

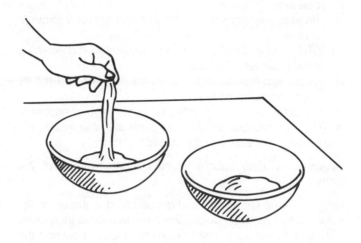

98. Spreader

Purpose To demonstrate diffusion of a gas.

Materials 1 teaspoon (5 ml) vanilla extract
large cotton ball
slender ½-pint (250-ml) jar with lid
timer
1-gallon (4-liter) jar with lid, or box about twice as tall as the small jar

Procedure

1. Pour the vanilla extract on the cotton ball.
2. Place the cotton ball in the small jar and secure the lid.
3. After 5 minutes, open the jar and note the odor of its contents.
4. Set the open small jar inside the large jar. Secure the lid on the large jar.
5. After 5 to 10 minutes, open the jar and note the odor of its contents.

Results Both the small and large jars smell like vanilla.

Why? The liquid vanilla extract **evaporates** (changes from a liquid phase to a gas phase), and the gas molecules produce the odor of vanilla inside the two containers. Gas molecules are so far apart that the cohesive force between them is very small. As a result, the molecules **diffuse** (spread apart and move freely in all directions). Their diffusion is limited only by their container.

99. Expando

Purpose To observe the effects of expanding gas.

Materials empty 2-liter plastic soda bottle
timer
½ cup (125 ml) tap water
1 tablespoon (15 ml) dishwashing liquid
saucer

NOTE: This experiment requires a freezer.

Procedure

1. Place the empty soda bottle in a freezer for 2 minutes or more.
2. While you are waiting, mix the water and dishwashing liquid together in the saucer.
3. Remove the soda bottle from the freezer and dip its open end in the soapy water.
4. Stand the bottle on a table and observe what happens.

NOTE: If a soap bubble does not form over the mouth, dip the bottle in the soapy water again.

Results A soap bubble forms over the mouth of the bottle.

Why? As the temperature of molecules decreases, molecular motion decreases and the cohesive force increases, pulling the molecules closer together. Cooling caused the air molecules inside the bottle to move closer together, allowing more air to enter the bottle. When the bottle was removed from the freezer, the cold air inside it heated up and the air molecules moved farther apart. Some of the air was forced out of the bottle and pushed on the soap film across the mouth of the bottle, making a soap bubble.

100. Foamy

Purpose To show how pressure affects dissolved gases.

Materials plastic cereal bowl
16-ounce (480-ml) glass soda bottle
¼ cup (63 ml) tap water
2 effervescent antacid tablets

Procedure

1. Set the bowl on a table and stand the soda bottle in it.
2. Pour the water into the bottle.
3. Break the antacid tablets in half.
4. Quickly drop the broken tablets into the bottle of water and immediately cover the mouth of the bottle with the palm of your hand.
5. Observe the contents of the bottle.
6. When it becomes difficult for you to keep your hand over the bottle because of the pressure against your palm, quickly lift your hand and observe what happens to the bottle's contents.

Results The antacid tablets mix with the water, producing bubbles. When the bottle is covered, bubbles are seen in the water and a small amount of foam forms on the surface of the water. Uncovering the bottle produces a bubbly foam that rises within the bottle.

Why? When the antacid tablets are combined with water, carbon dioxide gas is produced. Covering the opening of the bottle prevents the gas from escaping. As more gas is produced, the pressure inside the bottle increases. Increasing the pressure on any mixture of liquid and gas results in more gas dissolving in the liquid and a reduction in the size of the gas bubbles. Raising your hand allows the excess gas above the water to escape, which quickly reduces the pressure pushing down on the surface of the water. At this lower pressure, many gas bubbles move upward and break through the surface of the liquid. Each bubble rises, rapidly expands, and pushes some of the liquid upward, resulting in the rising foam.

101. New Stuff

Purpose   To demonstrate a chemical change.

Materials   Polident tablet
10-ounce (300-ml) clear plastic drinking glass
tap water
timer

Procedure
1. Observe the appearance of the tablet.
2. Fill the glass about one-half full with water.
3. Drop the tablet into the water and observe the results.
4. Allow the cup to sit for 3 to 5 minutes, then observe the contents of the glass.

Results   The tablet is green and solid when dry. When dropped in the water, it bubbles vigorously. After a few minutes, foamy green liquid is seen in the glass.

Why?   The solid tablet combines with liquid water to form a new substance, a gas. A process by which one or more substances are changed into one or more different substances is called a **chemical change**.

102. Speedy

Purpose   To determine how temperature affects the speed of a chemical reaction.

Materials   ¼ cup (63 ml) cold tap water
two 10-ounce (300-ml) transparent plastic
    drinking glasses
5 to 6 ice cubes
pen
masking tape
timer
spoon
¼ cup (63 ml) warm tap water
2 effervescent antacid tablets

Procedure
1. Pour the cold water into one of the glasses and add the ice cubes. Use the pen and tape to label the glass Cold.
2. Allow the water and ice to sit for 2 minutes, stirring periodically.
3. Use the spoon to remove the ice from the water. Discard the ice.
4. Pour the warm water into the other glass. Use the pen and tape to label the glass Warm.
5. Drop an antacid tablet into each of the glasses at the same time.
6. Don't stir. Observe the tablets to determine which dissolves first.

Results   The tablet in the warm water dissolves first.

Why?   In order for a chemical reaction to occur, the molecules of water must combine with the molecules on the surface of the antacid tablet. This combination occurs as the water molecules randomly collide with the molecules on the surface of the tablet. All particles of matter, such as the antacid tablets and the water, have **kinetic energy** (energy of motion). Kinetic energy increases with temperature. This means the water molecules in the glass of warm water are moving around at a faster speed than those in the glass of cold water. Thus, the rate of collision between warm-water molecules and antacid molecules is greater than that between cold-water molecules and antacid molecules. Thus, an increase in temperature increased the speed of the chemical reaction in this experiment. It might be inferred that this would be true for other chemical reactions.

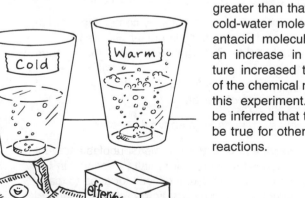

103. Brown Banana

Purpose To determine if vitamin C can inhibit oxidation.

Materials dinner knife
banana
2 saucers
2 sheets of typing paper
pen
3 vitamin C tables (100-mg tablets work well)
cutting board
rolling pin
timer

Procedure

1. Peel the banana, then slice it into 8 pieces.
2. Place 4 slices of banana in each saucer.
3. Set each saucer on a sheet of paper. Label one of the papers Without Vitamin C and the other With Vitamin C.
4. Place the vitamin C tablets on the cutting board and crush them with the rolling pin.
5. Using the dinner knife to scoop up the vitamin C powder, sprinkle the powder over the cut surface of the banana slices in the saucer labeled With Vitamin C.
6. Every 30 minutes for 2 hours or more, observe the color of each sample's surface.

Results The untreated banana slices slowly turn brown, but those covered with vitamin C are unchanged.

Why? Bananas and other fruit, such as apples and pears, discolor when bruised or peeled and exposed to air. This discoloration is cased by changes that occur when the cells are broken. The chemicals released by the damaged cells are **oxidized** (combined with oxygen), resulting in changes in the fruit. This process is called **oxidation.** Vitamin C is an **antioxidant,** a substance that **inhibits** (decreases or stops) oxidation. Covering the surface of the banana with vitamin C inhibits the discoloration caused by oxidation.

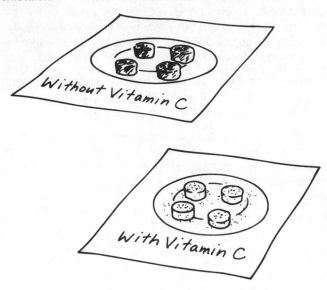

104. Soap Scum

Purpose To test for the hardness of water.

Materials 1 tablespoon (15 ml) distilled water
¼ teaspoon (1.2 ml) Epsom salts
small jar with lid
spoon
eyedropper
dishwashing liquid
timer
ruler

Procedure

1. Prepare a sample of hard water by combining the distilled water and Epsom salts in the jar. Stir well.
2. Add one drop of the dishwashing liquid to the jar, then secure the lid.
3. Shake the jar vigorously for 15 seconds.
4. Observe contents of the jar.

Results Few soap suds form above the water.

Why? The **hardness of water** is a measure of the amount of calcium, magnesium, and/or iron salts dissolved in the water. These substances make it difficult for soap to make suds. They combine with the **fatty acids** (chemicals found in animal and plant fat that are composed of carbon, hydrogen, and oxygen) in soap to form waxy, **insoluble** (unable to be dissolved) salts. Epson salts' chemical name is magnesium sulfate. The magnesium in the chemical combines with the fatty acids in the dishwashing liquid to form soap scum instead of soap suds.

105. Bubbler

Purpose To see how carbonates react to acids.

Materials long-handled spoon
  raw egg
  1 quart (1 liter) widemouthed jar white vinegar

CAUTION: Wash your hands after handling raw eggs. They can contain harmful bacteria.

Procedure
1. Use the spoon to place the egg in the jar, being careful not to crack the egg.
2. Fill the jar with vinegar.
3. Observe the appearance of the eggshell immediately and then periodically for the next 2 days.

Results Bubbles start forming immediately on the surface of the eggshell and increase in number over time. After about 2 days, the shell is no longer present, and a membrane, which is a thin, filmlike outer layer around the egg, holds the egg together.

Why? Chemicals containing combinations of carbon and oxygen with some other element, such as calcium, barium, or manganese, are called **carbonates.** The main ingredient of the eggshell is calcium carbonate. Vinegar is a mixture of water and an **acid** (a type of chemical that produces hydrogen ions—charged particles—when dissolved in water). When calcium carbonate combines with an acid, such as vinegar, new substances are produced, including carbon dioxide gas. The bubbles seen rising in the jar are carbon dioxide gas.

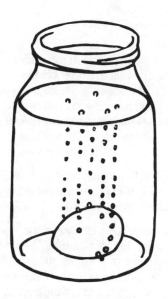

106. Clumped

Purpose To demonstrate the effect of calcium ions on milk coagulation.

Materials masking tape
  marking pen
  two 10-ounce (300-ml) clear plastic drinking
    glasses
  ½ cup (125 ml) skim milk in measuring cup
  ½ teaspoon (2.5 ml) Epsom salts
  2 spoons
  2 teaspoons (10 ml) vinegar

Procedure
1. Use the tape and pen to label the glasses A and B.
2. Pour ¼ cup (63 ml) of milk into each glass.
3. Add the Epsom salts to glass A and stir until it dissolves in the milk.
4. Using a separate spoon for each glass, dip a spoonful of milk out of each glass and compare their appearance.
5. Add 1 teaspoon (5 ml) of vinegar to both glasses.
6. Using the same spoons used in step 4 for each glass, stir to mix the vinegar and milk. Again, dip and compare the spoonfuls of milk.

Results The milk in glass B contains clumps. The milk in glass A does not have clumps.

Why? Vinegar, an acid, causes milk to **coagulate** (clump), such as happened in glass B. But the coagulation of milk can only happen if calcium ions (charged particles) are present in the milk. The milk in glass A did not coagulate because the Epsom salts reacted with the calcium ions to produce an insoluble calcium compound. The calcium ions were no longer present in the milk and thus could not cause coagulation.

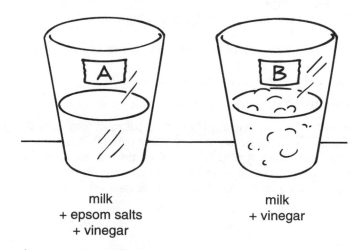

milk
+ epsom salts
+ vinegar

milk
+ vinegar

107. A New Look

Purpose   To observe a physical change.

Materials   4-inch (10-cm) circle of black construction
paper
saucer
1 tablespoon (15 ml) table sugar
magnifying lens
¼ cup (63 ml) tap water

Procedure

1. Place the black paper circle in the saucer.
2. Sprinkle a few crystals of sugar on the paper, and use the magnify lens to observe the sugar crystals.
3. Put all of the sugar in the cup of water. Stir until no sugar crystals are visible with your naked eye.
4. Dip out a spoonful of the liquid, and use the magnifying lens to look for sugar crystals in the water.

Results   When dry, the sugar crystals look like tiny white cubes. When the sugar crystals are mixed with the water, they are not visible.

Why?   The sugar crystals dissolve in the water. **Dissolving** is the process by which a **solute** (a material that dissolves) breaks up and thoroughly mixes with a **solvent** (a material in which a solute dissolves). Dissolving is a physical change that produces a **solution** (a combination of a solute and a solvent). A **physical change** is one in which the appearance of matter changes, but its properties and makeup remain unchanged. The sugar breaks into particles not visible even with the magnify lens, but they are still sugar.

108. Ink

Purpose   To produce a mixture.

Materials   red, blue, and yellow food coloring
4-inch (10-cm) square of waxed paper
toothpick
office paper

Procedure

1. Place 1 drop of each food coloring in the center of the waxed paper.
2. With the toothpick, stir the colors together. This will be your ink.
3. Using the toothpick, write your name on the office paper with the ink.
NOTE: Keep the ink for the next experiment.

Results   A dark ink mixture is formed.

Why?   The combination of the food colors is a mixture. A **mixture** is made of two or more substances that are physically combined. A **physical combination** is one in which the parts retain their separate properties and can be separated. (To separate the colors, see the next experiment.)

109. Separated

Purpose To separate the parts of a mixture.

Materials 3¼-inch (8.25-cm) basket-type coffee filter
round toothpick
ink from Experiment 108, "Ink"
timer
cup of tap water

Procedure

1. Stand the coffee filter upside down on a table.
2. Wet the end of the toothpick in the ink.
3. Touch the wet end of the toothpick to the center of the coffee filter to make a small dot of color.
4. Repeat steps 2 and 3 to make 8 to 10 small colored dots near the center of the coffee filter.
5. Allow the coffee filter to stand undisturbed until the ink on the paper dries. This should take 2 to 3 minutes.
6. Wet the tip of one finger in the water, then touch the center of the coffee filter.
7. Repeat step 6 twice, touching a different part of the paper so that all of the colored dots are wet by the water.
8. Without disturbing the paper, observe the colors on the paper periodically for 20 to 30 minutes.

Results The ink separates into three different colors: yellow, red, and blue.

Why? The method of separating the ink mixture into its parts is called **chromatography.** This method of separating is based on different factors, one of which is adhesive force. The color in the ink that has the least attraction to the paper moves fastest and farthest across the paper. The other colors move at slower speeds and shorter distances, and the one with the greatest attraction to the paper moves the slowest and the least. In this experiment, the blue color moved fastest and farthest, followed by yellow, then red.

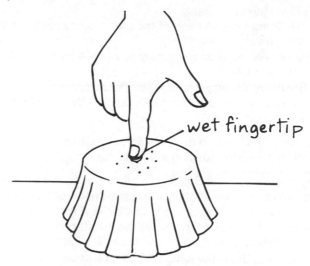

wet fingertip

---

110. The Same

Purpose To make a homogenous mixture.

Materials spoon
drinking glass
dishwashing liquid
tap water
paper towel
distilled water
1 teaspoon (5 ml) sugar
drinking straw

Procedure

NOTE: Never taste anything in a laboratory setting unless you are sure that there are no harmful chemicals or materials and that all containers are properly cleaned. This experiment is safe since only sugar and water are used.

1. Prepare the materials by washing the spoon and glass in soapy water.
2. Rinse the spoon and glass in clear water, and dry them with the paper towel.
3. Fill the cleaned glass half full with distilled water.
4. Add the sugar to the distilled water.
5. Stir until no sugar particles can be seen.
6. Stand a clean straw in the glass containing the sugar-water mixture.
7. Hold your finger on the top of the straw as you raise the straw out of the glass. (The sugar-water mixture stays

in the straw.) Place the bottom of the straw on your tongue. Taste the liquid, and make a mental note of its sweetness.

8. Use the straw to taste samples from the bottom, middle, and top of the sugar-water mixture.
9. Compare the taste of the three samples.

Results All three samples have the same sweet taste.

Why? Sugar and water form a special mixture called a solution. Solutions are produced by combining a solute with a solvent. The solute (sugar) dissolves in the solvent (water). The molecules in the crystals of sugar separate and move between the molecules of water. The sugar-water solution is **homogeneous,** meaning the solution is the same throughout. Samples of equal volume taken from the solution would contain the same number of sugar molecules and water molecules regardless of where the samples were taken.

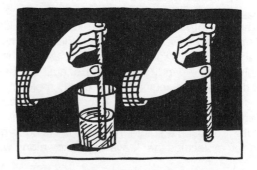

111. Sun Tea

Purpose   To determine how temperature affects how quickly a solute dissolves.

Materials   two 1-quart (1-liter) jars with lids
cold tap water
4 tea bags
timer

Procedure

1. Fill the jars with water.
2. Add 2 tea bags to each of the jars. Secure the lids on both jars.
3. At or near noon on a sunny day, set one jar outside in direct sunlight.
4. Set the remaining jar in the refrigerator.
5. Every 30 minutes for 2 hours, compare the color of the liquid in each jar.

Results   The liquid in the jar outside became dark more quickly than did the liquid in the jar in the refrigerator.

Why?   Heat from the Sun caused an increase in the temperature of the water in the jar that you put outdoors. Generally, a solute dissolves more quickly in a warm solvent than in a cold one. So the solute (the substance in the tea leaves) dissolved more quickly in the water warmed by the Sun, causing the water to become dark faster.

112. Pullers

Purpose   To demonstrate hydration.

Materials   10-ounce (300-ml) transparent plastic drinking glass
cold tap water
small piece of chocolate candy

Purpose

1. Fill the glass about three-fourths full with water.
2. Put the candy into the water.
3. Observe the area where the water touches the candy.

Results   Dark streams of material move away from the candy's surface.

Why?   When the candy (solute) is added to the water (solvent), it dissolves to form a solution. The dissolving of the candy occurs because water molecules randomly move about, colliding with the surface of the candy. While the cohesive force of the candy molecules holds them together, the adhesive force between the water molecules and candy molecules is great enough to pull the candy molecules off the candy's surface. Because of the attraction of the water molecules for the candy molecules, each of the freed candy molecules becomes completely surrounded by water molecules. This process by which water molecules surround a solute molecule is called **hydration.** The candy molecules that leave the candy along with their cluster of water molecules are said to be **hydrated** (surrounded by water molecules). As the surface layer of candy molecules is hydrated, the next layer is exposed to the water.

113. Plump

Purpose To demonstrate rehydration.

Materials 20 raisins
two 10-ounce (300-ml) clear plastic drinking glasses
tap water

Procedure
1. Place 10 raisins in each glass.
2. Fill one of the glasses with water. Observe the appearance of the raisins in each glass.
3. Allow the glasses to sit undisturbed overnight. During this time, observe the raisins in each glass as often as possible. Compare the size and shape of the raisins in each glass.

Results All the raisins look wrinkled at the start of the experiment. Over time, the appearance of the raisins in the glass without water does not change. But the raisins covered with water increase in size and their shape is more rounded.

Why? Raisins are made by **dehydrating** (removing water from) grapes. Before the dehydration process, grapes are round. Like all plants, grapes are made up of cells with rather stiff cell walls. When water is removed from the cells, the walls are generally not changed, but the cells collapse without the water to fill them. When the dehy-

drated fruit is placed in water, the cells fill with water and resume their original shape.

Reconstitution is the process of **rehydrating** (restoring water to) dried food, which means the cells of the food are returned to their original hydrated form. Rehydration doesn't return food to its exact original shape or taste.

114. Swollen

Purpose To demonstrate absorption.

Materials two 10-ounce clear plastic drinking glasses
2 Gummi Bears
timer

Procedure
1. Fill one of the glasses about three-fourths full with water.
2. Place a Gummi Bear in each glass.
3. Place the glasses where they will be undisturbed, but in view.
4. Observe the candy every hour for 6 or more hours.
NOTE: After the experiment is completed, discard the candy.

Results The candy in the glass without water remains unchanged, but the candy in the water swells.

Why? The process by which one substance takes in another, such as a sponge soaking up water, or as in this experiment, candy soaking up water, is called **absorption.** An increase in the volume of a substance is a good indication of absorption. Solids and liquids may also absorb gases. The candy in the glass without water did not noticeably change in size, so it can be assumed that either it did not absorb air, or the amount absorbed was not enough to make a visual difference in size.

115. Cleansing Power

Purpose To determine the cleansing effect of dishwashing liquid.

Materials
4 clear drinking glasses
tap water
masking tape
marking pen
three 1-teaspoon (5-ml)
  measuring spoons
cooking oil
dishwashing liquid
timer

Procedure

1. Fill each glass half full with water.
2. Use the masking tape and marking pen to number the glasses 1 through 4.
3. Use one of the spoons to add 1 teaspoon (5 ml) of cooking oil to glasses 2 and 4. Leave the spoon in glass 2.
4. Using a second spoon, add 1 teaspoon (5 ml) of dishwashing liquid to glasses 3 and 4. Leave the spoon in glass 4.
5. Place the third spoon in glass 3.
6. Stir the contents of glasses 2, 3, and 4 ten turns each.
7. Allow the glasses to stand undisturbed for 5 minutes.
8. Observe the appearance of the contents of each glass.

Results The contents of glasses 1 and 3 are clear. The contents of glass 2 have circles of oil floating on the surface, and those of glass 4 look cloudy.

Why? Glass 1 shows the appearance of water alone, which is clear. Glass 2 shows the appearance of a mixture of water and oil. The oil does not dissolve in the water, and soon after the stirring stops, the oil separates, forming a layer on top of the water. Glasses 3 and 4 contain detergent from the dishwashing liquid. Detergent molecules are long and have one end that attracts water and another end that attracts oil. Stirring the liquid in glass 4 breaks the oil into tiny droplets. Detergent molecules surround and attach to each droplet of oil. The outside of the detergent molecule attaches to water drops. The oil remains in tiny drops suspended throughout the glass of water but separated from the water by a protective coat of detergent molecules. This allows oily dirt to be removed from dishes and dissolved in the dishwater containing detergent. The dissolved oil clouds the water in glass 4. Because there is no oil in glass 3, the water remains clear.

DETERGENT MOLECULE

116. Sun-Dried

Purpose To use the Sun to separate salt from salty water.

Materials
cookie sheet
2 sheets of black construction paper
2 tablespoons (30 ml) table salt
1 cup (250 ml) tap water
spoon

Procedure

1. Cover the bottom of the cookie sheet with the black paper.
2. Add the salt to the water in the cup and stir. Most, but usually not all, of the salt will dissolve.
3. Pour the salty water over the paper. Try not to pour any undissolved salt onto the paper. Allow the undissolved salt to remain in the cup.
4. Place the cookie sheet in a sunny place where it will not be disturbed for several days. This can be by a window or outdoors if the weather is warm and dry.
5. Observe the paper daily until it is dry.

Results A thin layer of white crystals forms on the paper. A few small, white, cubic crystals form after several days.

Why? As the Sun heats the salty water, the water evaporates and dry salt is left on the paper. This experiment is similar to a method used by some salt companies to produce salt by the evaporation of water from seawater.

117. Icy

Purpose To determine why ice pops are softer than ice.

Materials 1-quart (1-liter) jar
tap water
2-quart (2-liter) pitcher
0.15-ounce (4.3-g) package of unsweetened flavored powdered drink mix
1½ cups (375 ml) granulated sugar
spoon
two 3-ounce (90-ml) paper cups
plate
2 craft sticks
freezer

Procedure

1. Pour 1 quart (1 liter) of water into the pitcher.
2. Add the drink mix and the sugar to the water and stir.
3. Place the paper cups on the plate.
4. Fill one of the cups with tap water and the other cup with the drink.
5. Stand a craft stick in each cup.
6. Set the plate in the freezer.
7. The next day, remove the plate from the freezer.
8. Peel the paper cup away from the frozen liquids.
9. Holding the craft sticks, *carefully* try to bite into the ice pop (the frozen drink) and the ice (the frozen water).

NOTE: Use the remaining drink and 12 cups and sticks to prepare extra ice pops to eat later or share with friends.

Results The liquid drink and water both changed to solids, but the ice pop is not as firm as the ice. It is easier to bit into the ice pop than the ice.

Why? The water molecules in each liquid combine to form ice crystals that join together in a solid block. In the ice pop, the ice crystals are separated in some places by sugar molecules and other ingredients in the drink mix, forming smaller ice crystals. These smaller ice crystals make the ice pops easier to eat than the frozen water, which has larger ice crystals.

118. Thinner

Purpose To compare the viscosity of different liquids.

Materials thick book
cookie sheet
4 eyedroppers
4 liquids: water, hand cream, baby oil, baby lotion
helper

Procedure

1. Use the book to raise one end of the cookie sheet.
2. Fill each eyedropper with a different liquid.
3. With the assistance of a helper, place 1 drop of each liquid on the raised end of the cookie sheet at the same time.
4. Observe and compare how long it takes each of the liquids to roll down the cookie sheet. This measure is called the liquids' flow rate.

Results The flow rates will depend on the liquids used. In the author's test, the water moved the fastest, followed by the oil, then the lotion. The hand cream barely moved at all.

Why? Viscosity is a measure of how fast a liquid flows. The least viscous liquid, or the one with the least viscosity, will have the fastest flow rate.

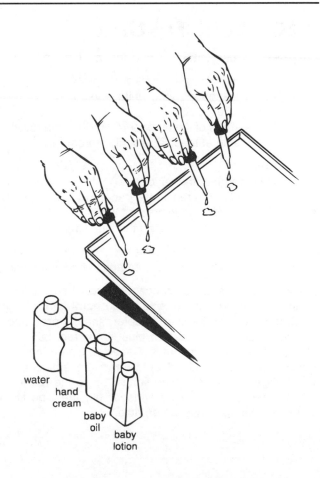

water
hand cream
baby oil
baby lotion

119. Flow Rate

Purpose To make and use a viscometer.

Materials scissors
   clear plastic dish detergent bottle with a pull top
   marking pen
   ruler
   modeling clay
   glass jar with a mouth slightly smaller than the upper part of the detergent bottle
   water
   timer
   adult helper

Procedure

1. Have an adult cut off the bottom of the detergent bottle.
2. Holding the bottle upside down, use the marking pen to make two short straight lines. Make the first line about 1 inch (2.5 cm) from the cutoff edge and the second line 4 inches (10 cm) from the first line.
3. Label the first line Start and the second line Stop. Close the pull top.
4. Place a ring of clay around the top edge of the jar's mouth, then stand the bottle upside down on the jar. Mold the clay ring so that the bottle stands upright, but do not secure the bottle with the clay.
5. Fill the bottle with cold tap water to about ½ inch (1.3 cm) above the start line.

6. Lift the bottle and pull the top open, then immediately set the bottle back on the jar.
7. When the water level reaches the start line, time how long it takes the water level to reach the stop line.

Results The flow rate varies depending on the bottle used. The author's flow rate for cold water was 39.3 seconds.

Why? A **viscometer** is an instrument that measures a liquid's viscocity. The amount of time it takes a liquid to flow out of a container depends on its viscosity. The viscometer can be used to measure flow rates of other liquids. Liquids with a low viscosity will flow faster than liquids with a high viscosity.

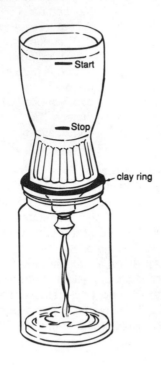

120. Acid Testing

Purpose To use litmus to test for the presence of an acid.

Materials 1 teaspoon (5 ml) white vinegar
   saucer
   2 strips of litmus paper: 1 red, 1 blue (available at teaching supply stores)

Procedure

1. Put the vinegar in the saucer.
2. Dip one end of the red litmus paper in the vinegar.
3. Observe any change in color of the paper.
4. Repeat steps 2 and 3, using the blue litmus.

Results The blue litmus turns red, but the red litmus does not change color (except perhaps to become redder).

Why? **Litmus** is a substance obtained from lichen, a plantlike organism. Litmus acts as a **chemical indicator,** which means it can be used to determine the presence of an acid or a base. Acids turn blue litmus red, but do not change the color of red litmus. **Bases** (a type of chemical that produces hydroxide ions) turn red litmus blue, but do not change the color of blue litmus. Since the red litmus did not change color in the vinegar but the blue litmus turned red, vinegar must be an acid.

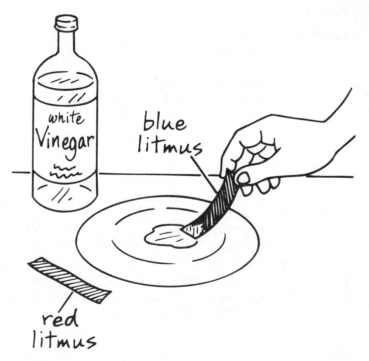

121. Base Testing

Purpose To use litmus to test for the presence of a base.

Materials spoon
½ teaspoon (2.5 ml) baking soda
1 teaspoon (5 ml) tap water
saucer
2 strips of litmus paper: 1 blue, 1 red (available at teaching supply stores)

Procedure

1. Use the spoon to mix the baking soda and water together in the saucer.
2. Dip one end of the blue litmus paper in the liquid.
3. Observe any change in color of the paper.
4. Repeat steps 2 and 3, using the red litmus.

Results The blue litmus does not change color (except perhaps to become bluer), but the red litmus turns blue.

Why? Bases are a type of chemical that turn red litmus blue but have no effect on the color of blue litmus. Since the red litmus turned blue in the baking-soda-and-water mixture but the blue litmus did not change color, baking soda must be a base.

122. Edible Acid

Purpose To identify an edible acid.

Materials saucer
strip of blue litmus paper (available at teaching supply stores)
½ lemon

Procedure

1. Lay the litmus paper in the saucer.
2. Squeeze a drop of lemon juice on one end of the paper.
3. Observe any change in the color of the litmus paper.

Results The blue litmus turns red.

Why? Since blue litmus turns red in an acid, lemon juice must be an acid. Lemon juice is an edible acid used in making foods, including lemonade and lemon pie.

123. Edible Base

Purpose To identify an edible base.

Materials 1 teaspoon (5 ml) distilled water
saucer
white antacid tablet
timer
strip of red litmus paper (available at teaching supply stores)

Procedure

1. Pour the water into the saucer.
2. Add the antacid tablet to the water. Allow the tablet to stand in the water for 5 minutes or more.
3. Dip the litmus paper in the water as close to the antacid tablet as possible.

Results The red litmus turns blue.

Why? Since red litmus turns blue in a base, the antacid tablet dissolved in water must be a base. An antacid tablet is a medicine taken for excessive stomach acid. The basic antacid tablet combines with an acid, and the results are chemicals that are **neutral,** which means they are neither an acid nor a base.

red litmus

Bubbly ANTACID Fast!

124. Heads Up

Purpose To simulate a nuclear change.

Materials hand towel   small empty coffee can
masking tape   100 pennies
marking pen   timer
bowl

Procedure

1. Lay the towel flat on a table.
2. Use the tape and marking pen to label the bowl Changed and the can Unchanged. Place all of the coins in the can.
3. Set the timer for 1 minute. At the end of 1 minute, pour the coins out of the can and onto the towel. (The towel keeps the coins from rolling off the table.)
4. Transfer half of the coins to the bowl. Record this as the first division.
5. Return the coins remaining on the towel to the can.
6. Repeat steps 3 to 5, halving the coins at the end of each minute and keeping track of how many divisions are made. If there is an odd coin, place it in the can. Stop when only 1 coin remains in the can.
7. How many times are the coins divided?

Results The coins are divided seven times.

Why? **Transmutation** is a process by which the nucleus of an atom changes so that a new element is formed. The change in the nucleus, called a **nuclear change,** results in the release of radiation (energy) and matter. An unstable nucleus is said to be **radioactive** (giving off radiation) and undergoes a breakdown called radioactive decay. Elements whose atoms undergo **radioactive decay** are called **radioactive elements.** The rate of decay of a radioactive element is called its **half-life** (the time it takes for half the atoms in a given sample of a radioactive element to decay). The half-life in this activity was 1 minute. At the end of 1 minute, half of the coins were placed in the bowl (changed). After about 7 minutes (seven divisions), all but one of the coins were in the bowl. In reality, it can take fractions of a second for some radioactive elements to decay, and thousands, millions, and even billions of years for other radioactive elements to decay.

IV
Earth Science

125. Wobbler

Purpose   To demonstrate Earth's precession.

Materials   drawing compass
  ruler
  index card
  scissors
  round toothpick
  adult helper

Procedure

1. Use the compass to draw a 2-inch (5-cm) circle on the index card.
2. Cut out the paper circle.
3. Ask your adult helper to use the point of the compass to make a tiny hole in the center of the circle.
4. Push the toothpick through the hole in the circle so that about ¼ inch (0.63 cm) of the toothpick sticks out one side.
5. Place the tip of the toothpick on a flat surface, such as a table, so that the long end of the toothpick is sticking up.
6. Quickly twirl the long end of the toothpick between your fingers, then let it go.
7. Observe the movement of the top of the toothpick.

Results   As the paper circle spins, the top of the toothpick moves in a circular path.

Why?   As the circle spins, there is a shifting of the weight because its shape is not perfectly round and the toothpick may not be exactly through the center of the paper. Earth's gravity pulls on the spinning circle, causing it to tip over and wobble. Earth, like the circle, wobbles as it rotates because it is not perfectly round. It has a slight bulge at the equator, making it larger around the equator than around from pole to pole. The gravity of the Sun and the Moon pull on Earth's bulging equator, making Earth wobble as it spins on its axis. Earth's axis moves in a circular path as the planet wobbles. This movement is called **precession**. The top of the toothpick makes many revolutions as the circle spins, but it takes about 26,000 years for Earth to wobble enough for its axis to make one complete turn.

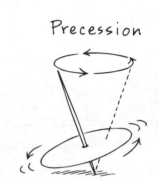

Precession

126. Opposite

Purpose   To demonstrate why the poles of Earth, as seen from space, appear to spin in opposite directions.

Materials   paper plate
  black marker
  sharpened pencil
  adult helper

Procedure

1. With the plate right side up, use the marker to label the right edge of the plate East and the opposite edge West.
2. Draw a curving arrow along the top edge of the plate, starting at West and ending at East.
3. Label the area near the center of the plate South Pole.
4. Turn the plate over so that the East label is on the underside of the right side. Label the right edge East and the opposite edge West as before.
5. Draw a West-to-East arrow along the *bottom* edge of the plate.
6. Label the area near the center of the plate North Pole.
7. Ask your adult helper to insert the point of the pencil through the center of the plate so the point exits the North Pole area.
8. Hold the pencil so that you are looking at the North Pole side of the plate. Rotate the pencil so the plate turns in the direction of the arrow. Note the direction, clockwise or counterclockwise, that the plate turns.

9. While rotating the pencil, raise the plate over your head so that you are looking at the South Pole side. Again note the direction, clockwise or counterclockwise, that the plate turns.

Results   As viewed from the North Pole, the plate turns in a counterclockwise direction. But viewed from the South Pole, the plate turns clockwise.

Why?   The plate, like Earth, rotates west to east. But the poles appear to spin in opposite directions—clockwise or counterclockwise. This is because the terms "clockwise" and "counterclockwise" are relative to the location of the observer.

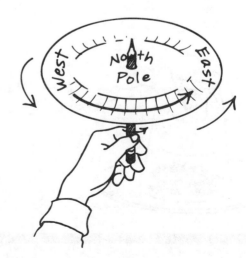

127. Flatter

Purpose To determine why the atmosphere is thinner at Earth's poles.

Materials drawing compass
ruler
4-inch (10-cm) square piece of poster board
marking pen
1-by-22-inch (2.5-by-55-cm) strip of poster board
transparent tape
one-hole paper punch
sharpened pencil

Procedure

1. Use the compass to draw a circle with a 2-inch (5-cm) radius on the square piece of poster board.
2. Use the ruler and pen to draw a line across the paper circle. Label the line Equator.
3. Overlap the ends of the strip of poster board about ½ inch (1.25 cm) and tape them together to make a loop.
4. Make a hole in the center of the overlapped ends of the loop with the paper punch.
5. Insert about 2 inches (5 cm) of the pencil through the hole in the loop.
6. Securely tape the front and back of the paper circle to the point of the pencil. The circle should hang in the center of the loop.
7. Holding the pencil between your palms, move your hands back and forth to make the pencil spin. Observe the shape of the spinning loop.

Results The middle of the spinning loop moves outward and the top and bottom of the loop flatten.

Why? Centrifugal force is the force that causes a spinning object to tend to move outward from the center. In this experiment, centrifugal force causes the middle of the paper loop to move outward. The top and bottom of the loop are then flattened. The paper loop represents the atmosphere around Earth. Earth's atmosphere is flatter and thinner at the poles and bulges at the equator because the atmosphere rotates with Earth. Since Earth rotates, it also bulges at the equator and is flatter at the poles. Because the atmosphere is not as thick at the poles, astronomers at the South Pole can more easily see through the atmosphere to study celestial bodies.

128. Zones

Purpose To make a model of Earth's temperature zones.

Materials drawing compass
ruler
12-inch (30-cm) square piece of white poster board
marking pen
scissors
pencil
4-by-8-inch (10-by-20-cm) index card
18-inch (45-cm) wooden dowel (Small-diameter rod works well.)

Procedure

1. Use the compass to draw a circle with a 6-inch (15-cm) diameter on the poster board.
2. Use the ruler and pen to draw a line across the center of the circle.
3. Draw four more lines parallel to the first line. Draw two of the lines 1½ inches (3.75 cm) above and below the first line, and the other two lines 4½ inches (11.25 cm) above and below the first line.
4. From top to bottom, label the lines Arctic Circle, Tropic of Cancer, Equator, Tropic of Capricorn, and Antarctic Circle.
5. Use the pencil and ruler to draw lines on the circle as shown. Use the index card to prepare a legend.
6. Cut out the circle, then tape the dowel to the middle of the back of the circle perpendicular to the lines.

NOTE: Keep this model of Earth for the next experiment.

Results You have made a model of Earth's temperature zones.

Why? Earth's four temperature zones, from coldest to warmest, are the Arctic Zone, the Antarctic Zone, the Temperate Zone, and the Tropical Zone. The coldest regions on Earth are the polar zones (Arctic and Antarctic Zones). The Arctic Zone lies between the Arctic Circle, at 66.5°N, and the North Pole at 90°N. The Antarctic Zone lies between the Antarctic Circle, at 66.5°S, and the South Pole, at 90°S. There are two Temperate Zones. These are areas of moderate temperature. One is between the Arctic Circle and the Tropic of Cancer, at latitude 23.5°N, and the other is between the Antarctic Circle and the Tropic of Capricorn, at latitude 23.5°S. The warmest region of Earth, called the Tropical Zone, is between the Tropic of Cancer and the Tropic of Capricorn.

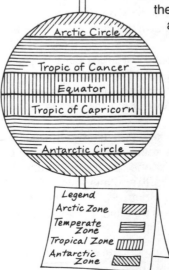

129. Seasons

Purpose To model the position of Earth relative to the Sun during the different seasons.

Materials marker
22-by-28-inch (55-by-70-cm) white poster board
Earth model from Experiment 128, "Zones"

Procedure

1. With the marker, draw a circle in the center of the poster board and label it Sun.
2. Label the edges of the poster board with these months in order—March, June, September, and December—starting with March to the left of the Sun and working counterclockwise around the board.
3. Lay the poster board on the floor so that its edges line up with the room's walls.
4. Stand next to the poster board so that March is to your right and you are facing the wall that lines up with December.
5. Holding the south axis of the Earth model in both hands, point the model's north axis toward the December wall. The north axis should be tilted slightly higher than the south axis.
6. Walk in a circle around the poster board in the order of the months, keeping your body and the dowel pointed toward the December wall. As you walk, slowly rotate the rod toward your right.

7. Note which month you are standing at when the North or South pole tilts toward the Sun.

Results The North Pole tilts toward the Sun when you are standing in front of June, and the South Pole tilts toward the Sun when you are standing in front of December.

Why? Earth rotates on its axis, and at the same time, it revolves around the Sun. This path of one celestial body around another is called an orbit. As Earth revolves about the Sun, its axis always points in the same direction. Since Earth's axis is tilted 23.5° in relationship to its orbit, from March to September, the North Pole is tilted slightly toward the Sun. This is when temperatures are warmest in the Northern Hemisphere and coldest in the Southern Hemi-

sphere. From September to March, the South Pole is tilted slightly toward the Sun. During these months, temperatures are warmest in the Southern Hemisphere and coldest in the Northern Hemisphere.

---

130. Rotation

Purpose To model a Foucault pendulum.

Materials metal washer
12-inch (30-cm) piece of string
marker
index card
swivel chair
ruler

Procedure

1. Tie the metal washer to the end of the string.
2. Draw an arrow lengthwise down the center of the index card.
3. Sit in a swivel chair and place the index card on your right leg so that the arrow is pointing away from you.
4. Hold the free end of the string so that the washer is about 6 inches (15 cm) above the arrow on the index card.
5. Start the washer swinging like a pendulum in the direction the arrow points, then keep your hand stationary as you slowly rotate the chair one turn. Rotate counterclockwise to demonstrate Earth's rotation at the North Pole, or clockwise for the South Pole. As the chair turns, observe the path of the pendulum in relationship to the direction the arrow points.

Results The swinging pendulum appears to move in the opposite direction to the rotating chair.

Why? The swinging pendulum changed direction very little, but the card moved because the chair rotated. The pendulum in this experiment represents a Foucault pendulum, named after physicist Jean Foucault (1819–1868), who first performed a pendulum experiment to show that Earth rotates. Foucault used a 223-foot (67-m) wire to suspend a sphere weighing 62 pounds (28 kg) from the dome of the Pantheon in Paris. The pendulum was free to move in any direction. A pin at the end of the pendulum made marks in sand on the floor. Because of **inertia** (a property

of matter that causes objects to resist any change in motion), the pendulum swung in the same direction as the pendulum in this experiment. But the marks in the sand were not in a straight line. They made a circular pattern. Since the sand rested on the floor of the building, and the building rested on Earth, the marks made by the pendulum showed that Earth rotates.

131. Shapely

Purpose To demonstrate how a lunar eclipse can indicate Earth's shape.

Materials tennis ball
masking tape
12-inch (30-cm) piece of string
4-inch (10-cm)-diameter circle of stiff paper
pencil
flashlight

Procedure

1. Suspend the tennis ball from the edge of a table by taping one end of the string to the tennis ball and the other end to the table.
2. Tape the circle to the end of the pencil.
3. In a darkened room, hold the flashlight on one side of the ball and the paper circle on the opposite side of the ball. Move the circle until the shadow of the ball falls across about half of the circle. Note the shape of the shadow.

Results A curved shadow is cast on the paper circle.

Why? The shadow of the ball is curved because the ball is round. The ball represents Earth, the flashlight the Sun, and the circle the Moon. Aristotle (384–322 B.C.) noted that the curved shadow of Earth on the Moon during a lunar

eclipse indicated that Earth is round. A **lunar eclipse** is an eclipse of the Moon that occurs when Earth comes between the Sun and the Moon so that Earth's shadow falls on the surface of the Moon.

132. Skinning Earth

Purpose To simulate the cutting of Earth's "skin" to form a flat map.

Materials knife (to be used only by an adult)
large orange
paper towel
marking pen
tracing paper
adult helper

Procedure

1. Ask your adult helper to use the knife to cut the skin of the orange into four equal sections from top to bottom.
2. Carefully peel off each section in one complete piece and press the outer skin faceup on the paper towel.
3. Following the four map patterns shown, draw the land-masses of Earth on the four separate pieces of orange peel.
4. Lay the pieces of orange peel side by side and observe how the landmasses fit together.
5. Lay the tracing paper over the orange peel and trace the shape of the land features, extending lines to make boundaries of continents continuous.

Results A flat map of a curved surface is produced.

Why? If you cut the "skin" of Earth into **gores** (long, pointed, elliptical sections) and lay them flat, as you did with the orange, you would have the most accurate map of Earth. Tracing the land features on the pieces taken from the orange left gaps in what are continuous landmasses.

Connecting the boundary lines distorted the actual shape and size of the land features. The amount of distortion is greatest at the poles and least at the equator.

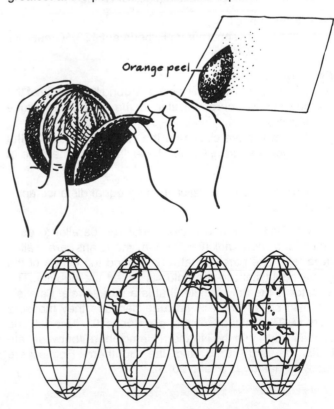

Orange peel

133. Great Circles

Purpose   To model meridians (lines of longitude).

Materials   lemon-size ball of modeling clay
pencil

Procedure
1. Shape the clay into a sphere.
2. Use the pencil to draw a circle around the center of the clay sphere.
3. Draw a second circle perpendicular to the first one.
4. Holding the sphere so that the lines cross at the top and bottom, observe the position of the lines and the distance between them (1) where the lines cross and (2) in the center of the sphere, midway between the top and bottom.

NOTE: Keep the clay sphere for the next experiment.

Results   The lines you drew in pencil are not parallel. They approach and cross each other at opposite ends of the sphere and are farthest apart around the center of the sphere.

Why?   The circles around the clay sphere are called **great circles** because the center of the circle and the center of the sphere are the same point. On a globe, a meridian is half of a great circle passing through the North and South Poles. The clay model has four meridians from pole to pole. While there is no limit to the number of meridians that

may be on a globe, many globes have 24. Meridians are also called **lines of longitude** because they measure longitude. A sphere has 360°. Longitudes 0° and 180° divide the globe into the **Eastern** and **Western Hemispheres.** To distinguish between longitudes in the Eastern and Western Hemispheres, the lines of longitude are labeled with an E or a W, such as 45°E or 45°W. Since longitudes 0° and 180° are boundaries for the two hemispheres, they are not labeled E or W.

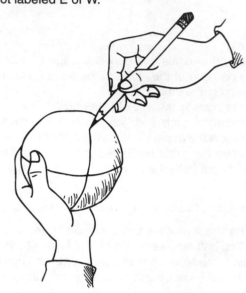

134. Side by Side

Purpose   To model parallels (lines of latitude).

Materials   pencil
clay sphere from Experiment 133, "Great Circles"

Procedure
1. Use the pencil to draw a circle around the middle of the clay sphere, perpendicular to the lines of longitude drawn on it.
2. Draw two more circles on the clay ball parallel to the line you just drew. Center these lines on either side of that line.

Results   You drew parallel lines an equal distance apart around the sphere.

Why?   Circles around a globe that run parallel to each other and perpendicular to the meridians are called **parallels.** The parallel that runs around the center of the globe equidistant to the poles is called the equator. The equator is the only parallel that is a great circle. Parallels are also called **lines of latitude** because they measure latitude. The latitude of the equator is 0°. This latitude divides Earth into the Northern Hemisphere (between latitudes 0° and 90°N) and the Southern Hemisphere (between latitudes 0° and 90°S).

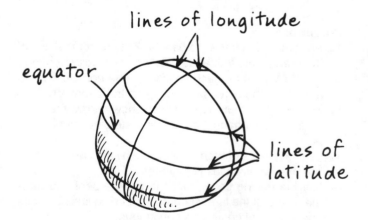

135. Model

Purpose To produce a 3-D model of a mountain.

Materials apple-size ball of clay
sheet of typing paper
metric ruler
pencil
about 30 toothpicks

Procedure

1. Break off a grape-size piece of clay and set it aside. Use the remaining clay to mold a mountain with smooth sides.
2. Set the clay mountain in the center of the paper.
3. Insert the zero end of the metric ruler in the grape-size piece of clay, then stand the ruler vertically next to the clay mountain.
4. On one side of the clay mountain, use the pencil and the ruler as a guide to draw a straight vertical line from the top of the mountain to its base.
5. Hold a toothpick horizontally across the 1-cm mark on the ruler, then insert the end of the toothpick into the line on the clay at this spot. Repeat this procedure at each centimeter mark until you reach the top of the mountain.
6. Turn the mountain one-quarter turn and repeat steps 4 and 5. Repeat the procedure two more times so that heights are marked on four sides of the mountain.

NOTE: Keep the model for the next experiment.

Results A mountain model with different heights indicated is made.

Why? In this experiment, you made a 3-D model of a mountain. The toothpicks are placed at different heights to indicate **elevation** (the height above sea level) of points on the mountain.

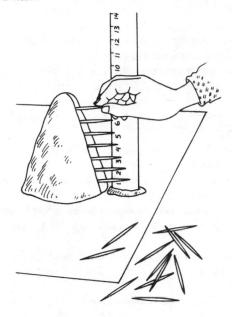

136. Loops

Purpose To produce a topographic map of a mountain model.

Materials mountain model from Experiment 135, "Model"
sheet of typing paper
pen
18-inch (45-cm) piece of dental floss

Procedure

1. Set the clay model in the center of the paper. Use the pen to trace around the base of the mountain. Make a mark on the paper at the base of each vertical line on the model.
2. Wrap the piece of dental floss around the mountain at the 1-cm height, letting the floss rest on the toothpicks. Cross the ends of the floss, then pull them in opposite directions to cut through the clay model.
3. Lift the top section of the clay straight up, remove the bottom slice, then lower the top section, matching the lines on the clay to the marks on the paper. Trace around the base of the clay.
4. Repeat steps 2 and 3 for the remaining heights.
5. Remove the top, final section of the clay mountain from the paper. Mark 0 cm, 1 cm, 2 cm, and 3 cm on the tracings as shown.
6. Observe the tracings on the paper.

Results Irregularly shaped, closed loops, one inside the other, are dawn.

Why? A **topographic map** is a flat map that uses **contour lines** (lines connecting points on Earth that have the same elevation) to show the shapes and heights of a land area. The closeness of the contour lines indicates the **slope** (the degree of steepness of an inclined surface) of the land. When the lines are far apart the slope is gentle, but when they are close together the slope is steep.

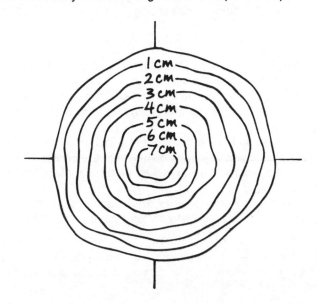

137. Spreader

Purpose   To demonstrate continental drift.

Materials   drawing compass   pie pan
ruler   tap water
sheet of typing paper   toothpick
pencil   dishwashing liquid
scissors

Procedure

1. Use the compass to draw a 4-inch (10-cm)-diameter circle in the center of the paper.
2. Use the pencil and the edge of the ruler to draw two intersecting lines, dividing the circle into four equal parts.
3. Draw a picture of the same dinosaur in each of the four sections.
4. Cut around the circle and along the lines to separate the four drawings.
5. Place the pie pan on a table and add enough water to cover the bottom of the pan.
6. Position the four pieces of paper as close together as possible to form a paper circle on the surface of the water.
7. Wet one end of the toothpick with dishwashing liquid.
8. Put the wet end of the toothpick in the water in the center of the paper circle.

Results   The paper pieces quickly move apart in all directions.

Why?   The circle represents **Pangaea** (the single landmass that is believed to have existed during the age of the dinosaurs). Over millions of years, the landmass broke up into continents. The separating paper pieces are a sped-up model of the millions of years required for the landmasses of Pangaea to separate.

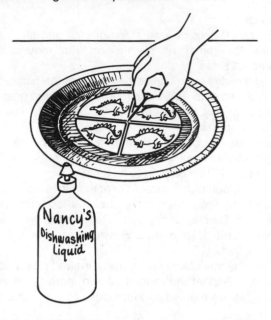

138. Dripper

Purpose   To demonstrate the water cycle.

Materials   ruler
tap water
transparent storage box about the size of a shoe box
plastic wrap
ice cube
resealable plastic bag
timer

Procedure

1. Pour 1 inch (2.5 cm) of water into the box and cover the top of the box with plastic wrap.
2. Put the ice cube in the bag and seal the bag. Place the bag in the center of the plastic wrap that covers the box.
3. Gently push the ice down about 1 inch (2.5 cm) so that the plastic wrap slopes down toward the center.
4. Set the box near a window so that the sunlight shines on the box.
5. Observe the underside of the plastic wrap below the ice cube every 20 minutes for 1 hour or until the ice melts.

Results   Water droplets form on the underside of the plastic wrap below the ice. Some of these droplets fall back into the water in the box.

Why?   The heat from the Sun provides energy, causing some of the liquid water in the box to evaporate. The water vapor rises, cools, and **condenses** (changes from a gas to a liquid) on the underside of the plastic, which has been cooled by the ice. As more water collects on the plastic, the droplets increase in size until their weight causes them to fall back into the water below. This is a model of Earth's **water cycle** (the natural process by which water from oceans, lakes, soil, and other sources on Earth evaporates, condenses in the atmosphere to form clouds, falls back to Earth in forms such as rain or snow, and returns to the oceans, lakes, and soil). The bottom of the box represents the surface of Earth, and the plastic represents Earth's atmosphere. As long as the box remains closed, the amount of water in the box remains the same; it just changes from one form to another.

139. Frosty

Purpose To demonstrate how frost forms.

Materials 7-ounce (210-ml) plastic drinking glass
ice
tap water
paper towel
4 tablespoons (60 ml) rock salt (used to make homemade ice cream)
timer

Procedure

1. Fill the glass three-fourths full with ice, then cover the ice with water.
2. Dry the outside of the glass with the paper towel, then sprinkle the salt over the ice.
3. Gently shake the glass back and forth four or five times to mix the ice, water, and salt.
4. Scratch the layer that forms on the outside of the glass with your fingernail every 15 seconds for 2 minutes. Observe the changes in the layer.

Results A very thin layer of soft white ice forms on the outside of the glass, usually during the first 15 to 30 seconds. The frosty layer of ice is thicker after 2 minutes.

Why? **Frost** is a light deposit of small, thin crystals of ice that form on cold objects when water vapor changes directly into a solid. Frost occurs when a layer of moist air comes in contact with a surface having a temperature below freezing (–32°F, 0°C). Salt lowers the temperature of the icy water below freezing, which cools the glass to a below-freezing temperature. The change from a gas directly to a solid without forming a liquid is called **sublimation.**

140. Stormy

Purpose To model the eye of a hurricane.

Materials 2-quart (2-liter) plastic bowl
tap water
scissors
string
ruler (the kind that has been punched for a three-ring binder)
paper clip
masking tape
black pepper
long-handled wooden spoon

Procedure

1. Fill the plastic bowl three-fourths full with water.
2. Cut the string so that it is 1 inch (2.5 cm) longer than the height of the plastic bowl. Tie one end of the string to the paper clip.
3. Thread about 1 inch (2.5 cm) of the free end of the string through the hole in the center of the ruler. Tape the end to the ruler.
4. Sprinkle pepper over the surface of the water in the bowl. Stir the water with the spoon in a counterclockwise direction a few times.
5. While the water is swirling, quickly suspend the paper clip in the center of the water. Try to drop the paper clip directly in the center of the spiral made by the swirling specks.

Results As long as the paper clip remains in the exact center of the swirling water, it moves slightly or not at all.

Why? The swirling water in the experiment represents a hurricane. A **hurricane** is a large tropical storm with winds of 74 miles per hour (118 kph) or more that rotate around a relatively calm center. The center of the swirling water in this experiment simulates the calm area in the center of a hurricane called the eye of a hurricane. The eye is a long, vertical tube of relatively motionless air in the middle of the storm.

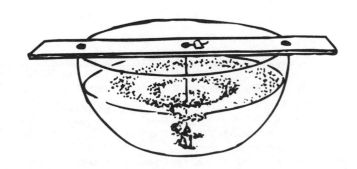

141. Raindrops

Purpose To measure the size of water drops.

Materials 1 cup (250 ml) flour
strainer
cake pan
spray bottle filled
    with tap water
large serving spoon

large bowl
sheet of construction
    paper, any dark color
pencil
metric ruler
magnifying lens

Procedure

1. Sift the flour through the strainer into the cake pan. Discard any flour particles that do not fall through the strainer.
2. Set the pan on a table, and spray a mist of water from the spray bottle so that it falls on the surface of the flour.
3. Use the spoon to scoop 1 to 2 spoonfuls of flour from the pan into the strainer. Scoop the drops of water along with the flour.
4. Hold the strainer over the bowl and gently shake it back and forth so that the flour falls through the holes in the strainer and into the bowl. Shake the strainer until all loose flour falls into the bowl and balls of flour remain in the strainer.
5. Pour the flour balls from the strainer onto the paper.
6. Repeat steps 3 to 5 until all the flour in the pan has been sifted and all the flour balls collected.

7. Measure the size of several of the flour balls, one ball at a time, by using the tip of the pencil to move each ball next to the ruler. Using the magnifying lens to see, move the ruler so that the left side of the ball is in line with a measuring mark.

Results A variety of different-size flour balls are formed.

Why? The water from the spray mist falls like raindrops on the surface of the flour. When the drops hit the flour's surface, fine particles of flour coat the outside of the drop. The flour coating on each water drop only slightly increases the size of the drop of water. Thus, the flour ball can be measured to determine the approximate size of the drop inside it.

142. Wet and Dry

Purpose To make a thread hygrometer.

Materials scissors
ruler
1-by-2-inch (2.5-by-5-cm) rectangle of poster
    board
one-hole paper punch
hammer
two size 3 finishing nails (Any small-head nail
    about 1 inch, 2.5 cm, long will work.)
2-by-4-by-12-inch (5-by-10-by-30-cm) board
    (Size of board is not critical.)
silk thread (available where embroidery floss
    is sold)
pen
protractor

Procedure

1. Make a pointer by cutting a triangle with a 1-inch (2.5-cm) base and a 2-inch (5-cm) height from the poster board. Use the paper punch to cut two holes along the height of the triangle. Make one hole near the base and the other near the tip.
2. Hammer a nail into the board about 1 inch (2.5 cm) in from one corner.
3. Hang the pointer on the nail by the hole near the base.
4. Tie one end of the silk thread to the other hole in the pointer. Hold the free end of the thread against the

board so that the base of the pointer is parallel to the edge of the board. Hammer the second nail into the board near the end of the strand, and tie the strand to the nail.
5. Use the pen and protractor to make six to eight marks at 5 intervals in an arc around the tip of the pointer.
6. Observe the position of the pointer on humid and dry days.

Results The pointer moves up on dry days and down on wet days.

Why? You have made a thread **hygrometer,** an instrument that can be used to indicate changes in **humidity** (the amount of water in the air). The thread expands when the humidity increases and contracts when the humidity decreases. The expansion and contraction of the thread lowers and raises the pointer.

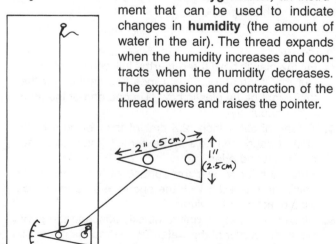

143. Coiled

Purpose To make a paper hygrometer.

Materials 1-by-10-inch (2.5-by-25-cm) strip of
newspaper
4-by-12-inch (10-by-30-cm) strip of aluminum
foil
transparent tape
scissors
short pencil about 6 inches (15 cm) long
1-quart (1-liter) jar with lid
thread spool
pen
writing paper

Procedure

1. Lay the newspaper strip in the center of the foil. Tape the paper to the foil with a single layer of tape along all edges of the paper.
2. Trim the foil edges, leaving about ¼ inch (0.63 cm) of foil around the paper on all sides.
3. Tape one end of the strip to the pencil below the eraser cap. Wind the strip snugly around the pencil so that the foil is on the outside.
4. Stand the writing end of the pencil in the hole in the thread spool, then set the spool inside the open jar.
5. Observe the strip periodically for several days, noting how tightly it is coiled around the pencil on dry and humid days.

Results The paper is more loosely coiled on humid days than on dry days.

Why? The newspaper is **hygroscopic,** which means it absorbs water from the air. As the pores in the paper fill with water, the paper expands and pushes against the foil, which is not hygroscopic. The force of the expanding paper causes the coil to unwind. The paper coil acts as a hygrometer. The higher the humidity, the more water available for the coil to absorb and the more the coil expands.

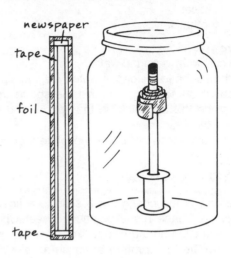

144. Changed

Purpose To demonstrate how rusting weathers a rock.

Materials cup
tap water
rubber gloves
lemon-size steel wool pad without soap (available at stores that carry painting supplies)
saucer
clear plastic drinking glass

Procedure

CAUTION: Steel wool can splinter. Wear rubber gloves when handling steel wool.

1. Fill the cup half full with water.
2. Put on the rubber gloves, then dip the steel wool pad into the cup of water. Hold the steel wool above the cup and allow the excess water to drain into the cup.
3. Place the moistened steel wool on the saucer, then invert the glass and stand it in the saucer so that it covers all of the steel wool.
4. Place the saucer where it will not be disturbed for 5 days. Each day, put on the rubber gloves, pick up the steel wool, and rub the wool between your fingers. Observe what happens to the steel wool.

Results Each day, more of the steel wool turns reddish brown and crumbles when touched.

Why? In the presence of water, oxygen in the air combines with the iron in the steel wool pad to form iron oxide, commonly called **rust. Rusting** (the process by which a substance rusts) is a type of **chemical weathering** (the breakdown of rocks by changes in their chemical composition). The rust weakens the structure of the steel wool, like the structure of rocks, causing it to fall apart when touched.

145. Meltdown

Purpose   To model how rocks melt.

Materials   cup
warm tap water
spoon
timer
½-by-½-inch (1.25-by-1.25 cm) square of
milk chocolate candy
saucer
toothpick

Procedure

1. Fill the cup with warm tap water.
2. Place the spoon in the cup of water.
3. After about 30 seconds, remove the spoon from the water, place the chocolate in the spoon, and set the spoon on the saucer.
4. Use the toothpick to move the chocolate around in the spoon.

Results   The chocolate melts.

Why?   **Melting** is the change of a solid to a liquid as a Results of an increase in energy, such as heat. Chocolate is solid at room temperature, but like all solids, it melts when heated. The temperature at which a solid melts is called its **melting point.** The change in the chocolate from a solid to a liquid due to an increase in its temperature is

similar to the change of solid rock to **magma** (liquid rock beneath Earth's surface). Rocks have a much higher melting point than the chocolate. The tremendous heat at depths of about 25 to 37½ miles (40 to 60 km) below Earth's surface is great enough to melt rock.

146. Easy Flow

Purpose   To model how pressure affects the rock in the asthenosphere.

Materials   1-cup (250-ml) measuring cup
tap water
9-oz (270-ml) plastic drinking glass
1-tablespoon (15-ml) measuring spoon
10 tablespoons (150 ml) cornstarch
spoon
bowl

Procedure

1. Prepare the simulated "putty rock" (the layer below the crust): pour ¼ cup (63 ml) of water into the plastic glass. Add 1 level tablespoon (15 ml) of cornstarch and stir well. Continue adding cornstarch, 1 tablespoon (15 ml) at a time. Stir well after each addition. The mixture should be thick enough that it is very hard to stir. Add a few drops of water if all of the starch will not dissolve, or add a little starch if the mixture looks thin.
2. Set the bowl on a table. Hold the glass containing the putty rock in one hand, and tilt the glass slightly so that about half of the material flows slowly into the bowl. Observe how the material flows.
3. Use the spoon to scrape the rest of the material out of the glass and into the bowl. Observe how the material behaves when forced to move.

Results   The material flows easily out of the glass when not forced, but cracks and breaks if pressure is applied.

Why?   Earth's **crust** (outer layer) and the upper portion of its **mantle** (the layer below the crust) make up a layer called the **lithosphere.** Below the lithosphere is a portion of the mantle called the **asthenosphere.** In this zone, the rock making up the mantle behaves like both a liquid and a solid. Rock in the asthenosphere is thought to behave like the simulated putty rock prepared in the experiment—it flows easily if moved slowly, but thickens and breaks if pressure is applied. This ability of a solid material to flow is called **plasticity.**

147. Layering

Purpose To simulate how deposited sediments form layers in the bottom of a lake.

Materials ½ cup (125 ml) each of 3 different colors of aquarium gravel
3 bowls
1½ cups (375 ml) soil or sand
spoon
2-quart (2-liter) rectangular glass baking dish
tap water
timer

Procedure

1. Pour one color of gravel into each of the three bowls.
2. Add ½ cup (125 ml) of soil or sand to each bowl of gravel. Use the spoon to mix the gravel and soil thoroughly.
3. Fill the baking dish half full with water.
4. Use your hand to slowly sprinkle the gravel-and-soil mixture from one of the bowls into the water. Wait 10 minutes and observe the appearance of the materials in the dish.
5. Sprinkle the gravel-and-soil mixture from one of the remaining bowls into the water. Again wait 10 minutes and observe the appearance of the materials.
6. Add the remaining gravel-and-soil mixture. After 10 minutes observe the contents of the dish.

Results The three different-colored mixtures form separate layers in the dish.

Why? **Regolith** is the loose, uncemented rock particles, including soil, that cover Earth. **Sediments** are regoliths that have been transported by **agents of erosion** (substances that cause erosion: wind, water, and ice) and deposited in another place. The sediments in this experiment (gravel and soil) sank through the water to form layers. Because the mixtures of gravel and soil were added at 10-minute intervals, the bottom layer is relatively older and the top layer is relatively younger than the other layers. Layers of rock are believed to form in a similar manner, and like the gravel-and-soil mixture, each rock layer is laid down on top of the one beneath it. This is how scientists can tell the relative age of each layer.

148. Bobber

Purpose To determine if surface water moves with each wave.

Materials large, rectangular glass baking dish
tap water
scissors
ruler
drinking straw
timer
unsharpened pencil

Procedure

1. Fill the baking dish three-fourths full with water.
2. Cut about 1 inch (2.5 cm) from one end of the straw.
3. Place the small piece of straw in the center of the water in the dish. Wait about 30 seconds to allow the water to become calm.
4. With the unsharpened end of the pencil, tap the surface of the water at one end of the dish. Observe the straw and the surface of the water.

Results Waves start where the water is touched by the pencil, move to the opposite end of the dish, and return again. This back-and-forth movement of the waves may happen several times. While the waves are moving back and forth across the surface, the straw is moving up and down.

Why? A water wave is a disturbance on the surface of water that repeats itself. In waves, energy is transferred from one water molecule to the next. As the energy of a water wave moves forward, the water moves up and down, but there is only a slight horizontal movement of the water molecules. Thus, objects floating on the water's surface may move horizontally slightly, but mostly they bob up and down as waves pass through the water.

149. Rising

Purpose To show how global warming could raise sea level.

Materials 5-ounce (150-ml) paper cup
tap water
cereal bowl
ruler
lemon-size piece of modeling clay
timer

Procedure

1. Fill the paper cup with water and place it in a freezer overnight.
2. Tear the paper cup away from the ice, then stand the ice in the bowl.
3. Mold the clay into an island shape with a high center and a shore line that's about ½ inch (1.25 cm) thick. Place the clay island in the bowl and press it against the bottom of the bowl.
4. Add about ¼ inch (0.63 cm) of water to the bowl.
5. Observe the water level on the shore of your island every 20 minutes or so until the ice block melts. This will take about 2 hours.

Results The level of the water rises and may cover part of the clay's shoreline.

Why? As the ice warms, it changes from a solid to a liquid. This liquid water spreads out and mixes with the water in the bowl, causing the volume of the water to increase and the water level to rise. If **global warming** (an increase in the average temperature of Earth) is great enough, **polar ice** (large masses of ice in the arctic and antarctic regions) will melt, raising sea level and flooding coastlines. It is not certain whether global warming is part of a natural long-term geologic pattern or the result of mankind's impact on global climate. For example, some think the burning of **fossil fuels** (energy sources, including coal and natural gas, made of buried remains of decayed plants and animals that lived hundreds of millions of years ago), which increases the amount of carbon dioxide in the atmosphere, is causing the atmosphere to warm.

150. Tabletop

Purpose To model an antarctic iceberg.

Materials 12-by-18-inch (30-by-45-cm) piece of heavy-duty aluminum foil
tap water
saucer
2-quart (2-liter) transparent bowl
1 tablespoon (15 ml) table salt
spoon

Procedure

1. Make a shallow box out of foil:
   - Fold the foil in half three times to make a 4½-by 6-inch (11.25-by-15-cm) rectangle.
   - Fold up about 1 inch (2.5 cm) of each edge of the rectangle to make the sides of the box.
   - Fold the foil to one side at each corner so that it is snug against the sides of the box.
2. Fill the foil box with water.
3. Set the water-filled box on the saucer and put the saucer in the freezer for 3 hours or until the water in the box is completely frozen.
4. Fill the bowl three-fourths full with water, then add the table salt and stir.

5. Peel the foil box away from the ice.
6. Place the ice in the bowl. Observe the amount of ice above and below the surface of the water.

Results More of the ice is below the water's surface than above it.

Why? When water freezes, it expands. The density of icebergs is slightly less than the density of salty ocean water. As a result, the iceberg floats, with about six-sevenths of the iceberg below the ocean surface. Icebergs in the Antarctic are **tabular** (shaped like a tabletop) like the ice in this experiment. Antarctic icebergs are more abundant and much larger than those in the Arctic. It is not unusual for antarctic icebergs to be several miles long while arctic icebergs generally have lengths of about 600 feet (180 m).

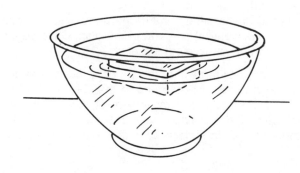

151. Patterns

Purpose   To demonstrate how atoms and molecules arrange themselves in minerals.

Materials   large, shallow baking pan
tap water
1 teaspoon (5 ml) dishwashing liquid
spoon
drinking straw

Procedure
1. Fill the pan half full with water, then add the dishwashing liquid. Gently stir.
2. Place one end of the straw beneath the surface of the water. Slowly and gently blow through the straw to make a cluster of 5 to 15 bubbles.
CAUTION: Only exhale through the straw. Do not inhale.
3. Move the straw to a different location and blow a single bubble.
4. With the straw, move the bubble so that it touches the bubble cluster.

Results   The single bubble attaches to the bubble cluster.

Why?   The bubbles represent the **chemical particles** of a mineral. Chemical particles are the atoms or molecules that make up minerals and matter. **Minerals** are substances found in the ground that do not come from living things, and have a definite chemical composition and a regular crystal form. The addition of the bubble to the bubble cluster represents the growth of a mineral crystal. Chemical particles, like the bubbles, can move around in a liquid. Just as a single bubble moves to a place where it fits in the bubble cluster, chemical particles dissolved in a liquid move to just the right spot in order to fit with other particles. Once a chemical particle like the bubble moves into the right place, it is held there by the attraction it has to the other chemical particles.

152. Overflow

Purpose   To make an instrument to determine specific gravity.

Materials   scissors
ruler
2-liter soda bottle
one-hole paper punch
flexible drinking straw
2-cup (500-ml) measuring cup
pitcher
tap water
adult helper

Procedure
1. Ask an adult to cut about 4 inches (10 cm) off the top of the soda bottle.
2. Use the paper punch to make a hole about 1 inch (2.5 cm) from the rim of the bottle.
3. Insert about ½ inch (1.25 cm) of the flexible end of the straw in the hole.
4. Bend the straw so that it forms a 90° angle. Place the measuring cup under the free end of the straw.
5. Use the pitcher to pour water into the bottle until it is just above the straw. Water will flow through the straw and into the cup.
6. When the water stops flowing into the cup, empty the cup, then set the cup in place under the straw. The water-filled bottle and the empty cup are your specific gravity instrument.
7. Push your fingers into the water in the bottle and note the amount of water that flows into the cup.
NOTE: Keep the instrument for the next experiment.

Results   The amount of water in the cup will depend on the size of your fingers.

Why?   **Specific gravity (S.G.)** is the ratio of the mass of a substance, such as your finger, compared to the mass of an equal volume of water. Your specific gravity instrument does not measure mass, but it does allow you to determine the volume of water equal to the volume of an object being measured. This is done by collecting the water **displaced** (pushed out of place) by an object placed in the instrument.

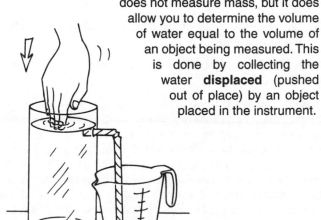

153. Heavy

Purpose To calculate the specific gravity of a mineral.

Materials 24-inch (60-cm) piece of string
fist-size sample of quartz, or any mineral of comparable size
food scale that measures in grams
writing paper
pencil
specific gravity instrument from Experiment 152, "Overflow"

Procedure

1. Tie the string around the mineral, then place the mineral on the scale to determine as accurately as possible its mass in grams (g). Record the mass.
2. Repeat steps 5 and 6 in "Overflow."
3. Holding the mineral by the string, slowly lower it into the bottle. Do not let the water spill over the rim of the bottle.
4. When the water stops flowing into the measuring cup, record the amount of water in the cup in milliliters (ml). Use the following example to determine the specific gravity (S.G.) of your mineral specimen:
   Example: A mineral with a mass of 150 g displaces 60 ml of water.
   - specific gravity (S.G.) = mass of mineral divided by mass of water displaced by mineral
   - mass of mineral = 150 g
   - volume of displaced water = 60 ml
   - 1 ml of water has a mass of 1 g, so the mass of displaced water = 60 g
     S.G. = 150 g ÷ 60 g
     = 2.5

Results The specific gravity of the mineral in the example is 2.5.

Why? Mass is measured with SI unit of grams. It has been determined that 1 pound of weight, a measure of the gravitational force between two objects, on Earth is equal to a mass of 454 g. Scales indicating gram units have been designed to show the mass of a given weight. To calculate specific gravity, divide the mass of the mineral by the mass of the water displaced by the mineral. The answer tells you how many times more massive or heavier the mineral is than water. The mineral in the example is 2.5 times as heavy as water. Most minerals have a specific gravity greater than 1, meaning that they are heavier than water. Every substance has a certain specific gravity, thus the specific gravity of a mineral or any substance can be a clue to its identity.

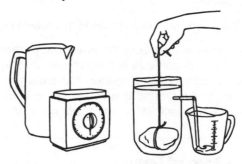

---

154. Scratch

Purpose To use a method for determining the hardness of a mineral.

Materials sharpened No. 2 pencil

Procedure

1. Hold the pencil against a table with one hand.
2. With your other hand, scratch the pencil lead with a fingernail.
3. Observe the ease or difficulty of making a scratch in the pencil lead.

Results Your fingernail easily cuts a groove in the pencil lead.

Why? The **hardness** of a mineral is its resistance to being scratched. Frederick Mohs (1773–1839), a German chemist, arranged ten common minerals into a hardness scale. He gave the softest mineral, talc, the number 1, and the hardest mineral, diamond, the number 10. The hardness value of a mineral is determined by how easily it can be scratched when rubbed by another mineral or material of known hardness. The rule is that a mineral can scratch any mineral or material with a lower hardness number. Your fingernail has a hardness of about 2½. Since your nail can scratch the graphite-and-clay mixture that makes up the pencil lead, the hardness of the graphite-and-clay mixture must be less than 2½.

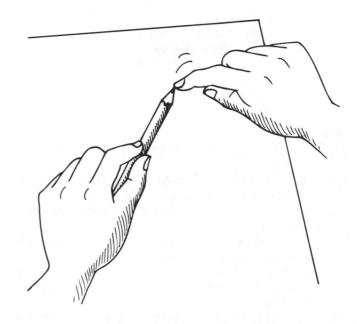

155. Powdered

Purpose To use a method for determining the streak of a mineral.

Materials piece of gypsum
sheet of very fine sandpaper

NOTE: White school chalk is not a mineral but can be substituted for gypsum in this experiment if gypsum is not available.

Procedure
1. Rub the gypsum back and forth across the sandpaper three or four times.
2. Observe the color of the streak made by the gypsum on the sandpaper.

Results The color of the streak is white.

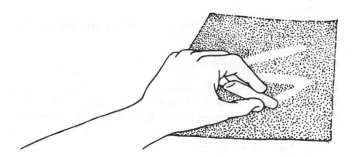

Why? The sandpaper is harder than the gypsum. Rubbing the gypsum across the rough, hard surface of the sandpaper removes fine particles of gypsum. These particles produce the white streak on the paper. Thus, the **streak** of a mineral is the color of the powder left when the mineral is rubbed against a rough surface that is harder than the mineral. The color and the streak of gypsum are the same, but this is not true for all minerals. Since a mineral's streak can be different from its color, its streak is used for identification.

156. Smooth

Purpose To model cleavage of a mineral.

Materials sheet of newspaper

Procedure
1. Hold the sheet of newspaper with both hands so that your thumbs meet in the center along the top of the sheet.
2. Tear the sheet of paper in half from top to bottom.

Results The paper tears in a relatively straight line down the page.

Why? One of the ways a mineral breaks is by cleavage. **Cleavage** is the property of a mineral that allows it to break along a flat smooth area called a **cleavage plane.** Along the cleavage plane, the bonds between atoms are relatively weak. (**Bonds** are forces that link atoms, groups of atoms, or molecules together.) The fibers making up a sheet of newspaper are generally lined up from the paper's top to its bottom. Tearing the paper from top to bottom breaks the lined-up fibers apart in a relatively straight, smooth line, much like breaking a mineral along a cleavage plane breaks the mineral apart, exposing two smooth edges.

157. Zigzag

Purpose To model fracturing of a mineral.

Materials sheet of newspaper

Procedure
1. Hold the sheet of newspaper with both hands so that your thumbs meet in the center along one side of the sheet.
2. Tear the sheet of paper in half from one side to the other.

Results The paper tears in a zigzag line.

Why? Fracturing is the breaking of a mineral across a cleavage plane, exposing uneven or jagged edges. Since the fibers of a newspaper generally line up from top to bottom on the sheet, tearing the sheet from side to side cuts across these lines of fibers. The result is a jagged tear, much like what happens when a mineral is broken across its cleavage plane. Paper is easily torn along or across its cleavage plane. But, it is more difficult to fracture a mineral than to cleave it. This is because the bonds are stronger between atoms that are not in line with the cleavage plane.

158. Stretched

Purpose To model the effect of tension on rock.

Materials 4 golf ball–size pieces of modeling clay, each a different color

Procedure
1. Shape each ball of clay into a piece about 2 inches (5 cm) wide, 4 inches (10 cm) long, and ¼ inch (0.63 cm) thick. Stack the pieces to make one big piece with four layers.
2. Hold the ends of the clay and slowly pull outward. Observe the shape of the clay as it is being pulled.

Results The layers of clay stretch, making the center section thinner.

Why? The different layers of clay represent **strata** (layers of one kind of rock material) of rock in the ground. Pulling on the clay layers models **tension,** a type of **stress** (a deforming force) by which rocks are stretched or pulled apart. This occurs when the strata are pulled apart during an **earthquake** (a sudden movement or shaking of Earth's crust).

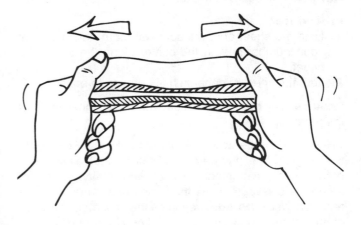

159. Hot Rocks

Purpose To model how igneous rock is formed.

Materials deep bowl
strainer large enough to fit across the bowl
4 sheets of construction paper—2 white,
   1 blue, 1 red
food blender (to be used only by an adult)
4 cups (1 liter) tap water
2 teaspoons (30 ml) white school glue
timer
10 to 12 sheets of newspaper
adult helper

Procedure
1. Set the strainer across the mouth of the bowl.
2. Tear one sheet of white and blue construction paper into small pieces.
3. Drop the paper pieces into the blender, then add half of the water and glue to the blender.
4. Ask an adult to turn on the blender and thoroughly mix the paper and water. A thick paper mulch will be produced.
5. Pour the paper mulch into the strainer over the bowl, and let it sit undisturbed for about 20 minutes.
6. After 20 minutes, fold 5 to 6 of the newspaper sheets in half and lay them on the table. Pick up the wet paper mulch with your hand and place it on top of the newspaper.
7. Allow the paper mulch to dry and solidify. This may take 2 to 3 days.
8. Repeat steps 1 through 7, using the remaining materials. *NOTE: Keep the dry mulches for the next experiment.*

Results The two colors of mulch, blue and pink, become lumpy solids.

Why? The blending of different-colored paper pieces and water represents the melting of different rocks beneath the surface of Earth due to heat and pressure. This melted rock is called magma. When magma rises to the surface of Earth, it is then called **lava**. Magma and lava cool and solidify to form a type of rock called **igneous rock**. The drying of the paper mulches represents the cooling of magma or lava to form igneous rocks.

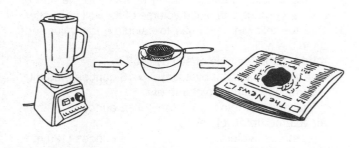

160. Transformed

Purpose To model the transformation of igneous rock into sedimentary rock.

Materials 2 mock igneous rocks from Experiment 159, "Hot Rocks"
10 to 12 sheets of newspaper
white school glue

Procedure
1. Break half of the pink rock into small pieces and lay the pieces in a thin layer on top of the newspapers.
2. Cover the top of the broken pieces of pink rock with glue, then press the pieces together with your hands.
3. Make a second layer, using pieces from half of the blue rock. Again, cover with glue and press the two layers together.
4. Add a third and fourth layer, alternating the pink and blue rocks.
5. Allow the material to dry. This may take 2 hours or more.

Results A solid form with alternating layers of colored mock rock is made.

Why? Igneous rock, like all rocks, can be transformed into **sedimentary rock** (rock formed by deposit of sediments). First, rocks are **eroded** (worn away), which means they weather, forming small particles that are moved by agents of erosion, including wind and rain. These particles are called sediment (represented by broken pieces of the mock rocks). Newly deposited sediment don't fit together tightly, so the spaces fill up with water, which often contains minerals (represented by the glue). More layers of sediment are added (represented by other layers of mock rock and glue). The weight of the layers presses on underlying sediments, compacting them. Compaction squeezes the water out, leaving minerals that glue the sediments together. This process of rock layer formation is called **cementation** (represented by the drying of the glue).

161. Spacey

Purpose To determine how soil texture affects the amount of air in soil.

Materials spoon
1 cup (250 ml) coarse soil
2-cup (500-ml) measuring cup with ounce measurements
tap water
writing paper
pencil
1 cup (250 ml) fine soil

Procedure

1. Use the spoon to add 8 ounces (240 ml) of coarse soil to the larger measuring cup. Do not press against the surface of the soil as you gently add the soil to the cup.
2. Slowly add 8 ounces (240 ml) of water to the cup of soil. Record the combined volume of the soil and water.
3. Use the following example to calculate the volume of air in the soil:
   total volume (volume of soil by itself
      + volume of water by itself)   = 16 ounces (480 ml)
   – combined volume (volume of
      soil and water in cup)   = 12 ounces (360 ml)
   air volume (total volume –
      combined volume)   = 4 ounces (120 ml)
   There are 4 ounces (120 ml) of air in the coarse soil.

4. Repeat the procedure, using the fine soil. Compare the air volumes.

Results The coarse soil has more air than the fine soil.

Why? The particles of coarse soil are larger. All soil particles are irregular in shape, and as they stack together there is space between them, which fills with air. Larger soil particles have more space between them. When soil and water are mixed, the air between the soil particles is displaced by water. Thus, the larger or more coarse the soil particles, the more air the soil contains.

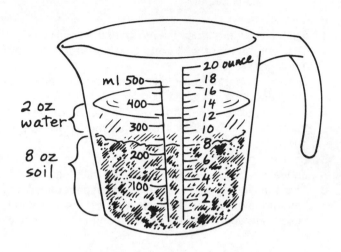

162. Crystals

Purpose To grow crystals.

Materials ¼ teaspoon (1.25 ml) dishwashing liquid
clear, transparent plastic folder
small paintbrush
1 tablespoon (15 ml) Epsom salts
clear drinking glass
1-tablespoon (15-ml) measuring spoon
tap water
spoon
writing paper
pencil

Procedure

1. Pour the dishwashing liquid onto the center of the plastic folder. Use the paintbrush to evenly spread the dishwashing liquid over the surface of one side of the folder. Allow the dishwashing liquid to dry.
2. Place the Epsom salts in the glass, then add 3 tablespoons (45 ml) of warm water and stir until all of the salt dissolves.
3. Place 3 tablespoons (45 ml) of the Epsom salts solution on top of the dried detergent layer. Use the bowl of the spoon to spread the solution as evenly as possible over the folder's surface.
4. Observe and record the changes that occur. If the air is dry and warm, the results take about 30 minutes. A longer time is required in cold and/or humid air.

5. Look through the folder toward a light. Notice and record the shape of the crystals.

Results Fans of long, clear, needle-shaped crystals form on the surface of the folder.

Why? As the water evaporates, the Epsom salts molecules move closer together and bond, forming long, needle-shaped crystals. The shape of the Epsom salts crystals reflects the arrangement of the molecules in the solid. The molecules are arranged like building blocks that lock together, thus the shape of the molecules determines the shape of the resulting crystal. The dried dishwashing liquid provides a rough surface to which the crystals can stick.

163. Clusters

Purpose To grow large crystals.

Materials 1 cup (250 ml) Epsom salts
2 cups (500 ml) tap water
20 drops of food coloring
1-quart (1-liter) jar with lid
spoon
12-inch (30-cm) pipe cleaner
ruler
12-inch (30-cm) piece of waxed paper
pencil

Procedure

1. Combine the Epsom salts, water, and food coloring in the jar. Stir until as much Epsom salts as possible dissolves in the water.
2. Use the pencil to coil the pipe cleaner so that it forms a spiral about 1 inch (2.5 cm) shorter than the jar.
3. Dip the coil in the Epsom salts solution until it is soaked, then remove it and lay it on the waxed paper. Close the jar.
4. Allow the coil to dry for 2 to 3 days.
5. Wrap one end of the coil around the middle of the pencil. Remove the lid from the jar and lower the coil into the Epsom salts solution.

6. Place the uncovered jar where it will be undisturbed and at room temperature. Observe the surface of the coil periodically for 2 to 6 weeks.

Results Small crystals are seen at first, but these grow into clusters of larger crystals.

Why? As the water evaporates from the pipe cleaner, small crystals of Epsom salts cover its surface. The tiny crystals, called seed crystals, provide a surface to which Epsom salts in the water will stick. The crystals grow larger as more Epsom salts stick to the tiny crystals.

164. Disorderly

Purpose To demonstrate how sudden cooling affects crystal formation.

Materials small box with lid
marbles

Procedure

1. Cover the bottom of the box with a single layer of marbles. The marbles should fit together loosely.
2. Close the lid on the box and lift the box. Using both hands to hold the lid secure, shake the box vigorously up and down, then from side to side.
3. Quickly set the box on a table. Open the lid and observe the position of the marbles inside.

Results Shaking the box moves the marbles, leaving them in a disorderly arrangement.

Why? The movement of molecules of lava is symbolized in this experiment by the movement of the marbles as the box is shaken. Stopping the motion of the box, and thus the marbles, symbolizes sudden cooling. Rapid cooling doesn't give molecules time to move into orderly patterns before the liquid solidifies. This irregular organization of molecules results in the formation of small crystals or no crystals. Rocks formed when lava suddenly cools have small crystals or no crystals.

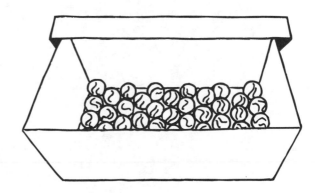

V
Physics

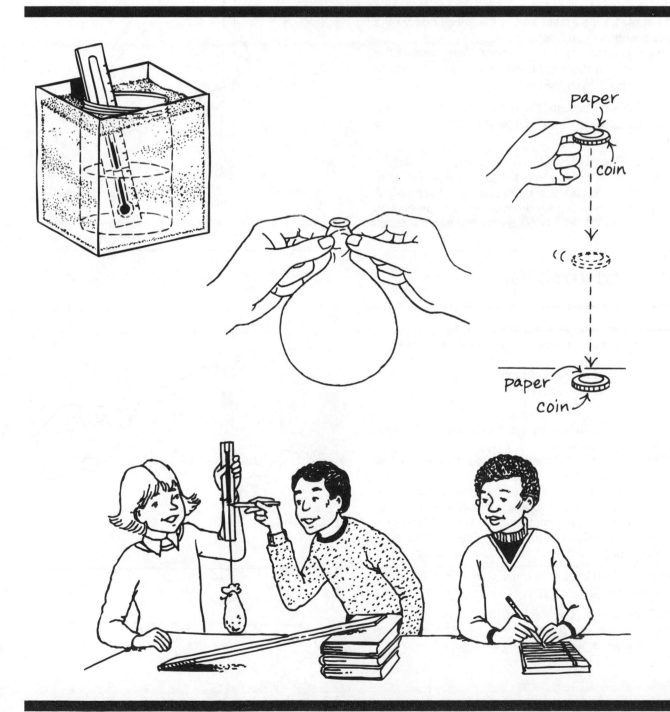

165. Moving

Purpose   To demonstrate inertia of a moving object.

Materials   sharpened pencil
walnut-size ball of modeling clay
marker
ruler

Procedure

1. Insert the point of the pencil into the clay ball. Use the marker to draw a line on the pencil where it meets the clay.
2. Holding the pencil vertically with the clay ball on top, raise the pencil about 2 inches (5 cm) above a table and firmly hit the eraser end of the pencil against the table seven to eight times.
3. Draw a second line on the pencil. Then remove the pencil from the clay and observe how much of the pencil was inserted into the clay.

Results   More of the pencil is in the clay after hitting the pencil on the table, and the clay covers the mark on the pencil.

Why?   The pencil and clay ball have **inertia,** a property of matter that causes objects to resist any change in motion. Because of inertia, objects tend to stay still if they are still and continue to move if they are moving. Only an outside force can change the inertia of an object. When the pencil and clay ball are moving, both have inertia of motion. Hitting the pencil against the table applies a force against the pencil, causing it to stop moving. But the inertia of the clay ball keeps it moving forward for a short time. So the clay pushes against the pencil point, causing the pencil to be pushed farther into the clay. The more securely the ball is attached to the pencil, the less the clay will move.

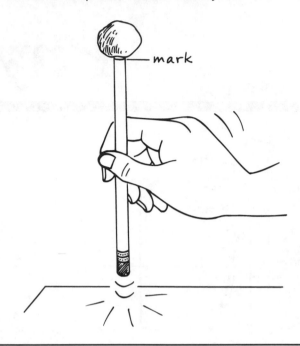

166. Immovable

Purpose   To demonstrate inertia of a still object.

Materials   fine-point black marker
2 pencils, 1 sharpened and with a new flat eraser
walnut-size ball of modeling clay
arrowhead eraser

Procedure

1. Use the marker to make a thin line just above the lead of the sharpened pencil.
2. Insert the point of the marked pencil into the clay ball so that the mark is just above the clay.
3. Place the arrowhead eraser on the other pencil.
4. Hold the marked pencil vertically in midair with the clay ball at the bottom. As you hit the flat eraser of this pencil with the arrowhead eraser of the other pencil 15 to 20 times, observe the marked area of the pencil.

Results   The black mark is not visible and more of the pencil is inserted in the clay.

Why?   Stationary objects tend not to move unless a force is applied to them. The pencil is being hit, but the clay ball is not. So the pencil moves into the stationary clay ball.

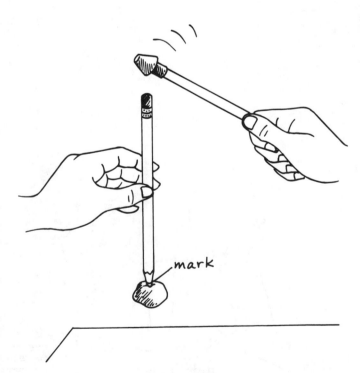

167. Scale

Purpose To make a scale.

Materials large rubber band
ruler
masking tape
paper clip
sharpened pencil
5-ounce (180-ml) paper cup
40 to 50 pennies (Any coins or small rocks will
   work.)

Procedure

1. Secure one end of the rubber band to the back of the zero end of the ruler with tape. Flip the other end of the rubber band over the face of the ruler.
2. Bend the paper clip into a hook. Attach one end of the hook to the rubber band.
3. Use the pencil to make a small hole beneath the rim of the paper cup.
4. Place the hook through the hole in the paper cup.
5. Hold the ruler vertically and observe the ruler measurement at the bottom of the rubber band.
6. Add coins to the cup 10 to 15 at a time until all the coins are used. Observe the ruler measurement at the bottom of the rubber band after each addition.

NOTE: Keep the scale for the next experiment.

Results The rubber band stretches and the ruler measurement increases as more coins are added to the cup.

Why? Gravity pulls things toward the center of Earth. Thus, gravity pulls the cup and the attached rubber band down. Coins have mass, which causes them to have weight in Earth's gravity. As the coins are added to the cup, the weight of the cup increases and the cup has a greater downward force. Thus, the cup pulls more on the rubber band, which stretches more. While your scale cannot give exact measurements, it can be used to compare the weights of objects.

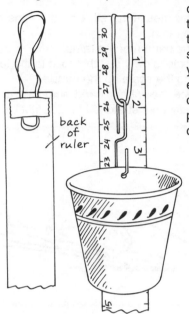

back of ruler

---

168. Straight Up

Purpose To determine the effort force needed to lift an object straight up.

Materials 3 books
1 cup (250 ml) uncooked rice
sock
12-inch (30-cm) piece of string
scale from Experiment 167, "Scale"
writing paper
pencil

Procedure

1. Stack the books on a table.
2. Pour the rice into the sock, and tie a knot in the sock.
3. Tie one end of the string to the end of the rubber band on the scale, and the other end of the string to the top of the sock.
4. Place the sock on the table, and lift the scale straight up until the bottom of the sock is level with the top of the stack.
5. Record the distance the rubber band stretches along the ruler.

NOTE: Keep these materials for the next experiment.

Results The rubber band stretches when used to lift the sock straight up. The distance the rubber band stretches varies depending on the type of rubber band used.

Why? **Work** is done when a force is used to move an object. The force you apply to do work is called **effort force.** In this experiment, gravity pulls the sock down, thus pulling the attached rubber band down. The weight of the sock is the measure of the gravitational force pulling it down. The distance the rubber band is stretched is equal to the distance any equal weight object would cause the rubber band to stretch. The amount of effort force needed to lift the sock is equal to the sock's weight.

169. Slanted

Purpose   To determine the effort force needed to lift an object using an inclined plane.

Materials   yardstick (meterstick)
setup from Experiment 168, "Straight Up"

Procedure

1. Place one end of the measuring stick on the edge of the books to make a ramp.
2. Place the sock on the bottom of the ramp.
3. Holding on to the scale, slowly pull the sock to the top of the ramp by sliding the scale up the ramp.
4. Observe the distance the rubber band stretches and compare it to the distance it stretched in "Straight Up."

Results   The rubber band stretches a shorter distance when used to pull the sock up the ramp than when lifting it straight up.

Why?   A **machine** is a device that makes work easier by changing the speed, direction, or amount of effort force applied. The **ramp** is a simple machine called an **inclined plane** (a flat, slating surface). It is used to raise an object with less effort force than it takes to raise the object straight up. The distance the rubber band stretched indicates that less effort force was needed to raise the sock up the ramp than was needed in Experiment 168, "Straight Up," to lift it straight up. Whether lifting the sock straight up or pulling it up the ramp, the results are the same: the sock is raised to the height of the books. It just takes less effort force when a machine is used to help do the work.

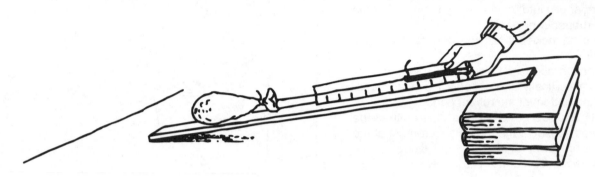

170. Lifter

Purpose   To demonstrate a first-class lever.

Materials   sturdy chair (The back should be as tall as the table.)
ruler
broom

Procedure

1. Place the back of the chair about 12 inches (30 cm) from the edge of the table.
2. Lay the broom handle over the back of the chair and under the edge of the tabletop.
3. Place your hand on the straw end of the broom and gently push down.

NOTE: Keep the setup for the next experiment.

Results   The straw end of the broom moves down and the other end rises, lifting the table.

Why?   A **lever** is a machine made of a rigid bar that turns around a **pivot point** called a **fulcrum** and is used to lift or move an object called the **load**. A **first-class lever** is a lever in which the fulcrum is between the two ends of the bar. This type of lever changes the direction of the force applied—one end of the lever moves up when the other is pushed down. It also generally requires less effort force to move a load with a first-class lever than with other types or without a lever.

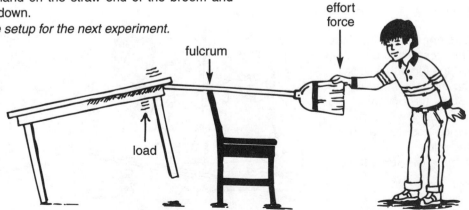

171. Longer

Purpose To determine how the position of the fulcrum of a first-class lever affects effort force.

Materials setup from Experiment 170, "Lifter"
yardstick (meterstick)

Procedure

1. Repeat the procedure for "Lifter," noting how much effort it takes to raise the table.
2. Repeat the procedure two more times, first with the chair 24 inches (60 cm) and then 36 inches (90 cm) from the table. Note the effort it takes each time.

Results The farther away the chair is from the table, the harder it is to lift the table.

Why? With a first-class lever, less effort force is used when the **effort arm** (the distance from the fulcrum to the point where you apply the effort force) is longer than the **load arm** (the distance from the fulcrum to the load). Thus, it was easier to raise the table (the load) when the chair (the fulcrum) was closer to the table.

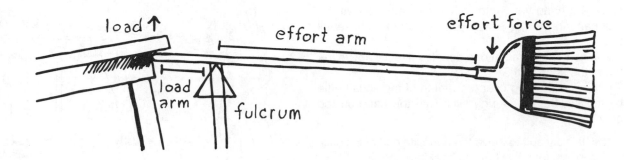

---

172. Second-Class

Purpose To demonstrate a second-class lever.

Materials 1-yard (1-m) piece of string
brick
yardstick (meterstick)
masking tape

Procedure

1. Tie one end of the string around the brick, and place the brick on the floor.
2. Holding the free end of the string, lift the brick about 6 inches (15 cm) above the floor. Note the effort required to lift the brick.
3. Place about 2 inches (5 cm) of the measuring stick on the edge of a table. Tape the end of the stick to the table.
4. Set the brick on the floor directly beneath the midpoint of the stick. Lower the free end of the stick, and tie the free end of the string around the center of the stick.
5. Lift the free end of the stick until the brick is about 6 inches (15 cm) above the floor. Again note the effort required to lift the brick.

Results It takes less effort to lift the brick by raising the end of the stick than by lifting it with the string.

Why? The measuring stick acts as a kind of simple machine called a **second-class lever.** A lever is considered second-class when the load (the object being moved—in this case, the brick) is between the fulcrum and the effort force (the force you applied to the stick). A second-class lever does not change the direction of the force; the load moves in the same direction as the effort force (the brick moved in the same direction as your hand—up). This type of lever, while not as effort-saving as a first-class lever, still requires less force to raise the load than if you lifted it without the lever.

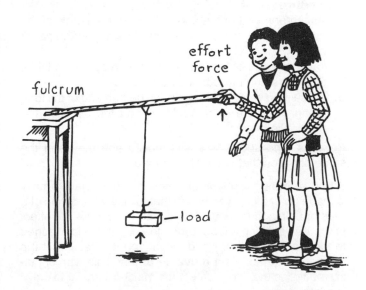

173. Ringer

Purpose   To demonstrate a third-class lever.

Materials   1-yard (1-m) piece of string
yardstick (meterstick)
metal screw ring for 1-quart (1-liter) canning
jars (Any metal ring with a 2½-inch, 6.4-cm,
diameter will work.)
glass soda bottle

Procedure

1. Tie one end of the string to the end of the yardstick (meterstick). Tie the free end of the string to the metal ring.
2. Stand the soda bottle on the floor.
3. Wrap one hand around the bottom of the stick, and place the hand you write with immediately above the first hand in the same way you would hold a baseball bat.
4. Stand so that the metal ring dangles directly above the top of the soda bottle.
5. Try to hook the ring over the mouth of the soda bottle by moving the measuring stick with the hand on top only.

Results   It is difficult to move the opposite end of the stick small distances; thus it is hard to hook the ring.

Why?   The measuring stick is used as a lever, with your writing hand applying the effort force while your other hand marks the point of the fulcrum. The ring is the load that is raised up and down. This is an example of a **third-class lever.** With a third-class lever, the effort force is always greater than the load force. Generally, the advantage of using a third-class lever is that it multiplies the distance of the effort force. The effort force needs to move only a small distance to move the load a large distance. but in this experiment, it is a disadvantage to use a third-class lever because the load only needs to be moved a small distance.

174. Movable

Purpose   To model the effect of using a movable pulley to lift a load.

Materials   12-inch (30-cm) piece of string
metal spoon
paper clip
masking tape
36-inch (1-m) piece of string

Procedure

1. Attach one end of the short string to the handle of the spoon, and tie the other end of the string to the paper clip.
2. Tape one end of the long string to the edge of a table. Run the string through the paper clip.
3. Raise the spoon by lifting up on the free end of the long string. Note the effort required and the direction the paper clip moves.

Results   The spoon is easily moved and moves in the same direction that you pull the string.

Why?   A **pulley** is a type of simple machine that normally is made up of a grooved wheel that turns by the action of a rope or belt in the groove. The paper clip models the effect of a pulley in lifting a load. Since the paper clip is attached to the load (the spoon) and moves in the direction of the effort force, it models a **movable pulley.** This type of pulley multiplies the effort force, thus making it easier to move the load.

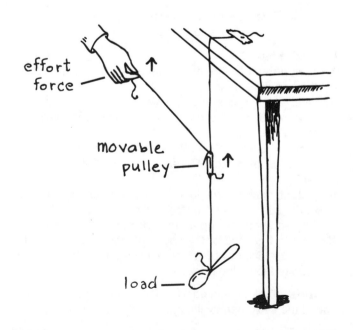

175. Weightless

Purpose To demonstrate apparent weightlessness.

Materials sharpened pencil
9-ounce (270-ml) paper cup
1-quart (1-liter) or larger plastic pitcher
tap water
helper

Procedure

NOTE: This activity should be performed outdoors in an area where water can be spilled. You may get wet when performing this experiment.

1. Use the pencil to punch a hole in the side of the paper cup near its bottom.
2. Fill the pitcher with water.
3. Ask your helper to hold the cup so that the hole points away from his or her body. Have your helper hold a finger over the hole as you fill the paper cup with water from the pitcher.
4. While sitting to the side of the cup, observe what happens when your helper removes his or her finger from the hole.
5. Again, have your helper cover the hole. Refill the cup.
6. As you watch from your sitting position, ask your helper to raise the cup as high as possible, then drop it.

Results When the cup is held stationary, the water streams out of the hole. But no water flows out of the hole while the cup is falling.

Why? Gravity pulls the water down out of the hole in the stationary cup. When the cup is released, gravity pulls both the cup and the water down. The cup and water fall together, thus the water does not flow out of the hole. Objects that fall only due to the pull of gravity are said to **free-fall**. During a free fall there is an apparent **weightlessness** (a state of having no weight). Astronauts in spacecraft orbiting Earth are free-falling because the craft and its contents are constantly falling around Earth. Astronauts and their spacecraft, like the cup and water, fall together and, therefore, cannot push against one another. Thus, they free-fall and the astronauts experience apparent weightlessness.

pitcher of water

176. Taller

Purpose To simulate the effect of gravity on a person's height.

Materials scissors
9-inch (23-cm) round balloon
small baby food jar
1-quart (1-liter) widemouthed jar

Procedure

1. Cut the balloon in half.
2. Stretch the bottom of the balloon over the baby food jar to cover its opening.
3. Place the covered baby food jar inside the larger jar.
4. Stretch the top half of the balloon over the mouth of the large jar so that the neck of the balloon is centered over the jar's mouth.
5. Push the stretched balloon down into the jar, allowing air from inside the jar to escape through the neck of the balloon.
6. Twist the balloon's neck, then pull it upward and observe the stretched balloon over the mouth of the baby food jar.

Results The balloon bulges upward

Why? The jars are used to simulate the effect of gravity on the movable disks in a person's spinal column. Pulling the balloon upward represents zero gravity, as shown when the rubber covering on the baby food jar bulges upward. In orbit, the height of astronauts increases because they are free-falling, which produces an effect of zero gravity on their bodies. On Earth, gravity pulls a person toward the center of Earth, but Earth pushes back, thus, the disks in the spinal column are pressed together. In free fall, gravity is pulling as before, but nothing is pushing back. The amount of gravity decreases with the altitude of the spacecraft. Thus, the disks separate, resulting in an increase in height. Skin and other body parts restrict the amount of disk separation.

177. Down?

Purpose   To show that gravity always pulls a free-hanging object down.

Materials   paper clip
12-inch (30-cm) piece of string
ruler
2 large books of equal height

Procedure

1. Tie the paper clip to one end of the string. Tie the free end of the string securely around the middle of the ruler.
2. Stand the books about 10 inches (25 cm) apart on a flat surface.
3. Support the ends of the ruler on the tops of the books. Observe the position of the string and paper clip.

Results   The paper clip hangs straight down.

Why?   Earth's gravity is the force that pulls objects toward the center of Earth. Thus, gravity pulls the free-hanging paper clip straight down. "Down" is toward Earth's center.

178. Paper Weight

Purpose   To determine if weight changes the falling rate of objects.

Materials   pencil
2 coins, 1 large and 1 small
office paper
scissors
yardstick (meterstick)

Procedure

1. Use the pencil and the small coin to draw a circle on the paper. Cut out the paper circle.
2. Hold the paper circle under the larger coin so that both are parallel with the floor. Be sure the paper does not extend past the edge of the coin.
3. Raise the coin and paper about 3 feet (1 m) above the floor, then release and allow both coin and paper to fall at the same time.
4. Observe the position of the coin and paper as they fall.
NOTE: Keep the coin and the paper circle for the next experiment.

Results   The coin and paper fall together. They separate only after hitting the floor.

Why?   Falling objects speed up the same amount each second, thus the lighter paper and the heavier coin both fall at the same rate. Gravity at or near Earth causes the speed of falling objects to increase at a rate of 32 feet per second (9.8 mps) for every second of falling time. The heavier coin pushes through the air with more force than does the lightweight paper circle, but because their falling rate is the same and they are positioned on top of each other, they move downward as if they were one object. Any separation of the pair upon striking the floor is the result of their bouncing on the surface.

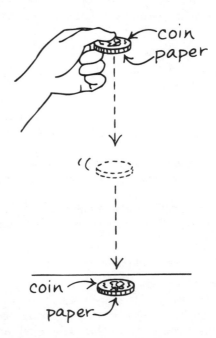

179. Reversed

Purpose To determine if changing the order of the falling coin and paper in "Paper Weight" would affect the results.

Materials coin and paper circle from Experiment 178, "Paper Weight"
yardstick (meterstick)

Procedure
1. Hold the paper circle on top of the coin so that both are parallel with the floor. Be sure the paper does not extend past the edge of the coin.
2. Repeat steps 3 and 4 of "Paper Weight," observing the position of the coin and paper as they fall.

Results The coin and paper fall together and separate only after hitting the floor.

Why? The heavier coin pushes through the air with more force than does the lightweight paper circle, and the two continue to fall at the same rate. When positioned on top of each other, they move downward as if they were one object regardless of which part of the pair is on top.

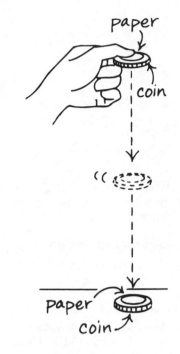

180. Lifter

Purpose To determine how air affects the falling rate of objects.

Materials pencil
coin
office paper
scissors

Procedure
1. Use the pencil and the coin to draw a circle on the paper. Cut out the circle.
2. Holding the coin in one hand and the paper in the other about 3 feet (1 m) above the floor, release the coin and paper at the same time.
3. Observe the position of the coin and paper as they fall.

Results The coin falls straight down and the paper floats back and forth through the air. The coin hits the floor first.

Why? All things would fall on Earth at the same rate of 32 feet per second (9.8 mps) if there were no air pushing on them. But air molecules in Earth's atmosphere push against falling objects and slow their falling rate. Heavier objects, such as the coin, push through the air with more force than do lightweight objects, such as the paper. The air pushing on the lightweight paper lifts and slows its falling rate. Thus, heavier objects fall through air faster than do lightweight objects.

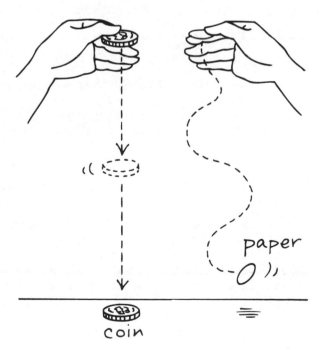

181. Free-Fall

Purpose   To determine the landing spot of free-falling objects.

Materials   scissors
ruler
two 5-ounce (150-ml) paper cups
masking tape
yardstick (meterstick)
glass marble

Procedure

1. Cut one cup down to a height of about 1 inch (2.5 cm), then tape the cup to one end of the measuring stick.
2. Tape the other cup to the stick about 4 inches (10 cm) away from the first cup.
3. Tape the other end of the stick to the door frame. The stick must be loose enough to be raised up and down easily.
4. Place the marble in the cut cup.
5. Holding on to the stick about 8 inches (20 cm) from the free end (just behind the taller cup), raise the stick until the cup end is about 21 inches (53 cm) from the floor.
6. Allow the stick to fall to the floor. At the moment you release the stick, give it a gentle push downward.
7. Repeat steps 4 to 6 several times, each time changing the force of the push, until the following results are achieved.

Results   The marble moves out of the cut cup and falls into the taller cup. If the marble did not fall into the cup, adjust the downward force on the stick. Push a little harder if the marble falls short of the cup; decrease the force of the push if the marble moves past the taller cup.

Why?   Free-falling objects are pulled straight down toward Earth's center at a rate of 32 feet per second (9.8 mps) for every second of falling time. The push on the stick gives it a faster falling rate than the rate of free-falling objects. The faster-moving stick pulls the cup out from under the marble. The unsupported marble free-falls toward the floor. The path of the falling stick places the taller cup under the falling marble.

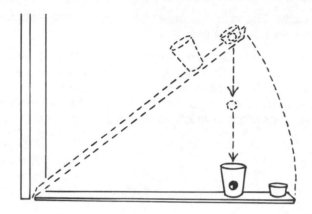

182. Magic Box

Purpose   To demonstrate center of gravity.

Materials   rock
small shoe box

Procedure

1. Place the rock in the inside corner of the shoe box, and close the lid.
2. Set the corner of the box that has the rock in it on the edge of a table. Be sure that no part of the rock is over the table's edge.

NOTE: If the box is difficult to balance use a larger rock.

Results   The box balances. Most of it is suspended over the edge of the table.

Why?   An object's **center of gravity** is the point at which the object's weight seems to be concentrated so that the object would balance if supported at this point. The weight of the rock causes the center of gravity of the box and its contents to be on the tabletop. So the box balances on the table's edge.

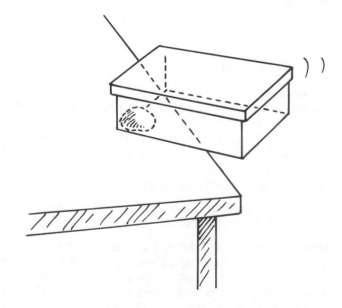

183. Balancing Point

Purpose To demonstrate balance.

Materials two 10-inch (25-cm) pieces of string
lemon-size piece of clay
ruler

Procedure

1. Make a loop in each string by tying the ends together in a knot.
2. Divide the clay into 3 equal parts. Squeeze one clay piece around the knotted end of each loop. Keep the third clay piece for a later step.
3. Place the loops on the ruler 2 inches (5 cm) in from each end.
4. Lay the ruler across your finger and move the ruler until it balances. Observe where your finger touches the ruler.
5. Add the third piece of clay to the clay on one of the loops.
6. Repeat step 4, observing where your finger touches the ruler this time.

Results At first, the ruler balances when your finger is at or near the middle of the ruler. When the extra clay was placed on one end, the ruler balanced when your finger was nearer the end with the larger clay piece.

Why? The place where the ruler balances on your finger is the center of gravity, which is the pivot point (the place about which an object turns). The downward force (weight) of each hanging clay piece pulls the ends of the ruler, causing them to turn in opposite directions, one clockwise and the other counterclockwise. **Torque** is the measure of the turning effect of each force and is determined by multiplying the force times its **torque arm** (the distance from the force to the pivot point). When the ruler balances, the torque on one side of the pivot point is equal to the torque on the opposite side.

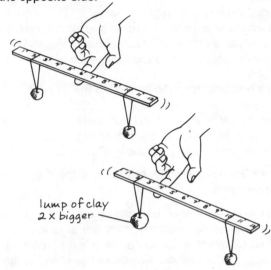

lump of clay
2 x bigger

---

184. Unbalanced

Purpose To demonstrate the effect of equal but opposite forces.

Materials sharpened pencil
4-by-6-inch (10-by-15-cm) piece of
    corrugated cardboard
2 paper brads
rubber band
4 round pens

Procedure

1. Use the pencil to make two holes through the cardboard, one at either end of one short side.
2. Secure a paper brad in each hole, then wrap the rubber band around the paper brads as shown.
3. Place the pens parallel to each other on a flat surface, such as a table or floor. Then set the cardboard on the pens, separating the pens as much as possible beneath the cardboard.
4. Hold the carboard with one hand. Stretch the rubber band toward the short side opposite the brads, forming a triangular shape as shown. Then release the cardboard and the rubber band. Observe what happens.

Results The rubber band moves forward and the cardboard moves backward.

Why? The motion of the cardboard can be explained by **Newton's third law of motion,** which states that for every action there is an equal and opposite reaction. When the stretched rubber band is released, it exerts an **action force** (a force applied to an object) on the cardboard. At the same time, the cardboard exerts a **reaction force,** which is a force equal to an action force, but in the opposite direction. When the rubber band is released, its action force is directed forward and the cardboard's reaction force pushes the cardboard in the opposite direction, or backward. These two forces are equal in magnitude, but opposite in direction.

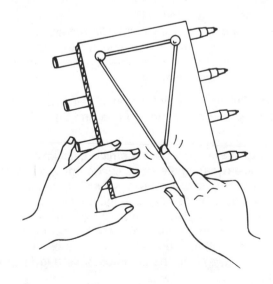

185. Balloon Rocket

Purpose To demonstrate how a rocket moves.

Materials   12-foot (3.6-m) or longer string
4-inch (10-cm) piece of soda straw
9-inch (22.5-cm) round balloon
masking tape
ruler
helper

Procedure

1. Thread the string through the straw.
2. Stretch the string across a room and attach the ends to the walls so that the string is taut and about waist high.
3. Inflate the balloon, squeeze it closed, and hold it under the straw.
4. Ask a helper to tape the balloon to the straw using two pieces of tape, each about 2 inches (5 cm) long.
5. Slide the straw and the inflated balloon to the end of the string that is nearer the mouth of the balloon.
6. Release the balloon and observe its motion.

Results The balloon and straw move along the string as the balloon deflates.

Why? The movement of the balloon, like that of a rocket, can be explained by Newton's third law of motion, which states that for every action force there is a reaction force. In the case of the balloon, the rubber pushes on the air inside, forcing it out the opening (an action force). The force of the air on the balloon (a reaction force) pushes the balloon in the opposite direction. Since the forces act on different materials (rubber and air), they don't cancel each other out. The same action-reaction forces move a rocket forward. The rocket pushes the gases downward (an action force) and the gases push the rocket upward (a reaction force).

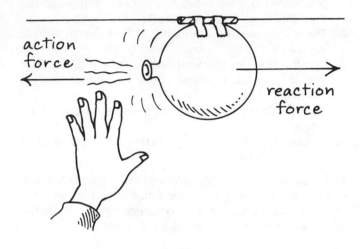

186. Dancers

Purpose To demonstrate how the buoyancy of a material can be changed.

Materials   1½ cups (375 ml) white vinegar
1-pint (500-ml) jar
2 quarter-size pieces of eggshell from a boiled egg
clock

Procedure

1. Pour the vinegar into the jar.
2. Break the eggshells into eight different-size pieces.
3. Drop the eggshells one at a time into the jar.
4. Observe what happens to the eggshells immediately and for the next few minutes.

Results Bubbles quickly form on the eggshells. Within 2 to 3 minutes, the shells start to rise and then sink in the liquid.

Why? Eggshells contain the chemical calcium carbonate. When calcium carbonate and vinegar mix, a chemical change occurs. One of the new chemicals produced is carbon dioxide gas. That's what is in the bubbles seen on the eggshells. These bubbles act like little life preservers and cause the shells to be **buoyant** (able to float in or on the surface of a fluid). As the shells rise, some of the bubbles get knocked away and the shell loses its buoyancy and sinks again.

187. Outward

Purpose To demonstrate the effect of centrifugal force.

Materials scissors
string
ruler
4 paper clips

Procedure

1. Cut a piece of string long enough to loosely tie around your waist. Tie the string around your waist.
2. Cut 4 more pieces of string, each about 18 inches (45 cm) long. Tie a paper clip to one end of each string.
3. Tie the free end of the 4 strings to the string around your waist. Space the strings as far apart as possible, but position them so that you can see them.
4. Standing away from objects and people, turn around quickly. Observe the movement of the strings as you turn.

Results The strings rise up and fly outward from your body.

Why? The force that causes a spinning object to tend to move outward from the center is called centrifugal force. Since the 4 strings in this experiment are attached to you yet free to move, and you are a spinning object, they move outward from your body because of centrifugal force.

188. Crawler

Purpose To demonstrate the effect of friction on motion.

Materials pencil
8-by-8-inch (20-by-20-cm) square of poster board
scissors
one-hole paper punch
36-inch (1-m) piece of string
ruler

Procedure

1. Draw a large turtle on the poster board. Cut it out.
2. Use the paper punch to make a hole at the top of the turtle's head.
3. Thread both ends of the string through the hole so that there is a loop in the string.
4. With the turtle on the floor, stand a chair leg in the loop.
5. Keeping the loop taut, move the turtle until the ends of the string extend about 6 inches (15 cm) from the hole.
6. Holding the ends of the string at a slight angle to the hole, pull one end at a time and observe the motion of the turtle.

Results When the ends are held at an angle, the paper moves forward each time the string is pulled.

Why? Holding the ends of the string at an angle increases the contact with the paper, which increases **friction** (the resistance of motion of two materials moving against each other). As the friction between the paper and the string increases, the string doesn't easily move over the paper. Instead, the resistance of the movement of the string across the paper results in the paper moving with the string as the string moves. Thus, the paper turtle appears to crawl toward the chair leg as the ends of the string are pulled.

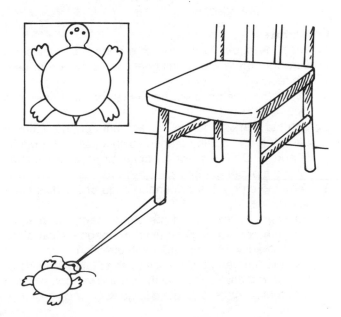

189. Breakable

Purpose To determine why eggs don't generally break under a bird.

Materials large bowl
small uncooked egg

Procedure

CAUTION: Wash your hands after handling raw eggs. They can contain harmful bacteria.
1. Set the bowl on a table. (This is just in case there is a flaw in the egg and it breaks.)
2. Hold the egg over the bowl lengthwise in the palm of your hand so that one of the rounded ends points toward your fingers. (Don't wear rings.)
3. Using only the hand that holds the egg, squeeze the egg as hard as you can.

Results You probably cannot break the egg.

Why? Pressure is the amount of force on an area. One way that pressure can be reduced is by applying force over a larger area. The dome shape of an eggshell spreads the pressure you applied over a larger area. In the same way, the weight of a bird's body is spread out and doesn't push hard enough in any one place to break the egg.

---

190. Pole Seeker

Purpose To identify the poles of a magnet.

Materials masking tape
office paper
directional compass
marking pen
6-inch (15-cm) piece of string
disk magnet

Procedure

1. Tape the paper to the top of a nonmetallic table. Be sure that there are no magnetic materials on or near the table.
2. Place the compass in the center of the paper and locate north.
3. Use the marking pen to make a mark on the paper at the north and south compass points. Label the marks N and S. Draw an arrow connecting the two marks. This is a paper compass.
4. Tape the string to the rounded edge of the disk magnet.
5. Holding the free end of the string, hang the magnet over the paper compass until the magnet's flat sides point steadily in a north-to-south direction.
6. Use the tape and the marking pen to label the side of the magnet that points north with a large dot, and the side that points south with a large X.

NOTE: Remove the string and keep the labeled magnet for the next experiment.

Results The poles of a magnet are identified.

Why? A compass needle is a magnet with a north and a south pole, or end. Near Earth's North Pole is a place called Earth's **magnetic north pole.** This is the place where the north end of a compass needle points. The south end of a compass needle points to Earth's **magnetic south pole,** near Earth's South Pole. If a magnet is allowed to swing freely, one pole, or end, will always point toward Earth's magnetic north pole and the other will point toward the magnetic south pole. The north-seeking end of the magnet is called the **north pole** of the magnet. The opposite south-seeking end of the magnet is called the **south pole** of the magnet.

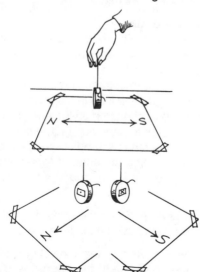

191. Push and Pull

Purpose   To observe the forces between two magnets.

Materials   labeled magnet from Experiment 190, "Pole Seeker"
another disk magnet of the same size
masking tape
marking pen

Procedure
1. Follow the procedure in "Pole Seeker" to label the second disk magnet.
2. Stand one of the magnets on edge on a nonmetallic table so that the X side faces you.
3. Hold the other magnet so that the X faces you, then move it near but not touching the magnet on the table. Observe the movement of the magnet on the table.
4. Turn the magnet in your hand around so that the dot faces you. Hold it close to but not touching the magnet on the table. Again, observe the movement of the magnet on the table.

Results   When the poles facing you are the same, the magnet on the table rolls away from the magnet in your hand. But when opposite poles face you, the magnet on the table rolls toward the magnet in your hand.

Why?   The poles of magnets exert two forces upon each other. These forces are attraction, which draws the poles together, and **repulsion,** which keeps the poles separate or apart. Magnetic poles attract each other when they are "unlike" (north and south), and repel each other when they are "like" (north and north, or south and south).

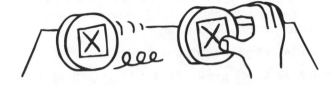

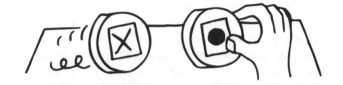

192. Force Pattern

Purpose   To produce a pattern that shows the magnetic field around a disk magnet.

Materials   scissors
12-inch (30-cm) pipe cleaner
disk magnet
index card
glue

Procedure
1. Cut the pipe cleaner into 16 equal pieces.
2. Place the magnet on a nonmetallic table and cover it with the index card, then spread a thick layer of glue over the area of the card that covers the magnet.
3. Hold one of the pipe cleaner pieces upright about ½ inch (1.25 cm) above the gluey card, then drop it straight down into the glue. Drop all of the pieces this way.
4. Leave the card undisturbed until the glue dries, which should take about 1 hour.

Results   The pipe cleaner pieces form a round flower-shaped design, with the outer pieces leaning outward at an angle and those in the center standing more vertically. The dried glue keeps the pipe cleaner pieces in place.

Why?   A **magnetic field** is the area of force around a magnet, in which the magnet affects the movement of some metal objects. The pipe cleaner pieces contain a thin steel wire, which is pulled toward the magnet when the wire enters the magnetic field. The arrangement of the pipe cleaner pieces indicates the direction of the lines of force in the magnetic field.

193. Whistler

Purpose To produce sound.

Materials 12-inch (37.5-cm) round balloon

Procedure
1. Inflate the balloon.
2. Holding the neck of the balloon between the first fingers and thumbs of both hands, slowly stretch the neck sideways as far as possible, forming a narrow opening which lets the air out slowly.

Results A high whistling sound is heard.

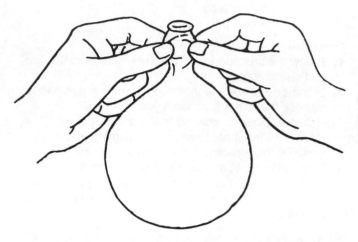

Why? As the air passes through the opening in the balloon's neck, the rubber vibrates, producing sound waves. As the rubber vibrates outward, the air molecules around the outside are compressed. But these air molecules have more space and spread apart when the rubber vibrates inward. The part of the sound wave where the air molecules are most dense is called an area of **compression,** and the area where the air molecules are least dense is called an area of **rarefaction.** One compression and one rarefaction make up a sound wave. Each time any part of the rubber moves back and forth, a sound wave is produced. As the rubber keeps vibrating, a train of sound waves move away from the balloon. The faster the rubber vibrates, the faster the sound waves are produced and the higher the **pitch** (how high or low a sound is) of the sound produced.

194. Pass It On

Purpose To demonstrate how sound energy travels.

Materials 5 or more dominoes
　　　　　　ruler

Procedure
1. Stand the dominoes about 1½ inches (3.75 cm) apart in a row.
2. Knock the first domino in the row over, then watch the movement of each domino.

Results The first domino falls and hits the second domino, which falls and hits the third, and so on.

Why? Sound travels in waves. The wave is produced when an object vibrates. With each vibration of the object, air molecules around the object compress, then spread out. Each time these air molecules compress, they push on the air molecules in front of them, causing this second group of air molecules to compress. The second group of air molecules push on a third group, and so on. It is sound energy that travels away from the vibrating object in all directions, not the air molecules. While sound energy caused by a vibrating object is passed on through the air in all directions around the vibrating object, the energy of the first falling domino in this experiment is passed from one domino to the next along a single row of dominoes. Also, unlike the dominoes, air molecules return to their original position once the energy has been passed along.

195. Sender

Purpose To determine which conducts sound best, a solid or a gas.

Materials sharpened pencil
two 7-ounce (210-ml) paper cups
36-inch (1-m) piece of string
2 paper clips
wire clothes hanger
metal spoon
2 helpers

Procedure

1. Use the pencil to make a small hole in the bottom of each cup.
2. Thread one end of the string through the hole in one of the cups. Knot the end of the string and attach a paper clip to the string between the knot and the cup as shown. Do this for the second cup also.
3. Ask one of your helpers to hold one cup while you hold the other. Walk away from your helper until the string is taut between the cups in your hands.
4. Ask your other helper to hang the clothes hanger on the middle of the string, then strike the hanger with the spoon. Note the sound produced.
5. Place your cup over your ear and instruct your helper to do the same.

inside of cup

6. Again, ask your second helper to strike the hanger with the spoon. Note the sound.

Results A soft clanking sound is heard at first, but with the cup over your ear, a loud bell sound is heard.

Why? The hanger vibrates when struck with the spoon. As the hanger vibrates, it pushes on the air around it, causing the air to vibrate. The vibrations (sound) produced by striking the spoon are conducted (sent from one place to another) through the air to your ear and you hear the sound. The sound is also conducted through the string. Holding the cup to your ear allows you to hear the sound that is conducted through the string. Air is a gas and the string is a solid. The difference in the sounds heard indicates that solids conduct sound much better than do gases.

---

196. Higher

Purpose To demonstrate the difference in pitch between open and closed wind instruments.

Materials scissors
ruler
drinking straw

Procedure

1. About 2 inches (5 cm) from the end of the straw, make a cut through about three-fourths of the straw. Do not cut the straw apart.
2. Bend the straw at the cut so the two sections are at a 90° angle to each other. This is a model of a wind instrument.
3. Place the end of the shorter section in your mouth and cover the end of the longer section with your index finger.
4. Blow through the straw and listen to the sound produced.
5. Remove your finger from the lower section and blow again. Compare this sound to the first sound.

NOTE: Keep the model for the next experiment.

Results The sound is higher when the end of the lower section of the straw is open.

Why? Each of the straw sections is a tube filled with a column of air. When you blow through the straw, the air inside moves forward, causing the air in the lower section

to vibrate. Air vibrates faster in an open tube than in a closed tube. Since a faster vibration produces a higher pitch, open tubes have a higher pitch than do closed tubes. In wind instruments, such as the trumpet, clarinet, French horn, and pipe organ, vibrations in columns of air produce sounds with different pitches. If the instrument is closed—for example, by covering the opening of a trumpet—a sound with a lower pitch is produced.

197. High and Low

Purpose To demonstrate how the length of the column of air in a wind instrument affects pitch.

Materials glass of water
wind instrument model from Experiment 196, "Higher"

Procedure

1. Set the glass of water near the edge of a table.
2. Hold the wind instrument as in step 3 of "Higher," but do not cover the end of the lower section with your finger.
3. Place the end of the lower section just below the surface of the water in the glass.
4. Blow through the straw while you lower and raise the straw in the water. Listen to the sound produced as the straw is moved up and down in the water.

Results The pitch of the sound is lower when the straw is lowered into the water and higher when it is raised.

Why? Blowing through the straw causes the column of air in the lower section to vibrate. The shorter the column of air, the faster the air vibrates. The faster the vibrations, the higher the pitch. The sound produced depends on the amount of air in the tube. When the tube is out of the water, it contains more air, so the column of air is longer.

When the straw is in the water, the column of air is shorter. As the column of air shortens, the pitch rises. Different-length tubes in wind instruments behave in the same way.

198. Louder

Purpose To demonstrate the effect of a megaphone on sound.

Materials marker
22-by-28-inch (55-by-70-cm) piece of poster board
yardstick (meterstick)
26-inch (65-cm) piece of string
pencil
drawing compass
scissors
transparent tape
helper

Procedure

1. Mark a dot in the center of one of the longer sides of the poster board, 14 inches (16.5 cm) from the corners.
2. Tie a loop in one end of the string.
3. Inset the pencil point through the loop, then place the point at one corner of the marked side of the poster board. Pull the string over the dot and hold the string on this dot with your thumb. Using the pencil and string as a drawing compass, draw a semicircle (half a circle) by moving the pencil across the poster board to the other corner of the marked side.
4. Using the actual compass, place its point on the dot and draw a semicircle with a diameter of 2 inches

(5 cm). Cut out this small semicircle, then cut out the larger semicircle.

5. Shape the cutout into a cone by overlapping and taping the straight sides. You have made a megaphone.
6. Give your helper instructions, saying, "Listen to what I am saying now and make a note of how loud my voice is."
7. Without changing the loudness of your voice, repeat step 6, but speak through the small end of the megaphone, directing the large open end toward your helper.

Results Speaking through the megaphone makes your voice sound louder.

Why? A **megaphone** is a device used to make a person's voice sound louder. Sound goes in the small end and out the larger end of the megaphone. The sound is louder coming out than going in because the megaphone points the sound waves in one direction and keeps them from spreading out in all directions. Thus, the sound waves coming out of the megaphone have more energy. As the energy of sound increases, its loudness increases.

199. Stickers

Purpose To produce static electricity.

Materials 20 to 25 pieces of puffed rice cereal
2-foot (60-cm) piece of plastic food wrap
sheet of notebook or office paper

Procedure
1. Put the pieces of cereal on a table.
2. Crumple the plastic wrap into a fist-size wad.
3. Quickly rub the wad of plastic back and forth across the sheet of paper 10 to 15 times. Immediately hold the plastic above the cereal pieces, near but not touching the cereal.

Results The cereal leaps up to the plastic.

Why? **Electricity** is a form of energy that comes from electric charges. Static electricity is the energy due to the buildup of electric charges on an object. These charges are called **static charges** because they are stationary (nonmoving). When two substances are rubbed together, such as the plastic and the paper, electrons are lost from one substance and gained by the other. Rubbing the plastic causes it to collect negative charges. When the negatively charged plastic approaches the cereal, the positive charges in the cereal are attracted to the negative charges in the plastic. This attraction is great enough for the lightweight cereal to move upward against the downward pull of gravity, and the cereal sticks to the plastic.

200. Lemon Power

Purpose To show how you can make a battery out of a lemon.

Materials wire cutters
ruler
18-gauge copper wire
(Larger-gauge wire will work.)
paper clip
coarse sandpaper
lemon
adult helper

Procedure
1. Ask your adult helper to strip 2 inches (5 cm) of insulation from the wire. Cut off the bare metal with the wire cutters. Keep the 2-inch (5-cm) piece of bare wire.
2. Then ask your adult helper to straighten out the paper clip and cut a 2-inch (5-cm) piece from one end. Keep the 2-inch (5-cm) piece.
3. Use the sandpaper to smooth any rough edges from the wire and the piece of paper clip.
4. Gently squeeze the lemon with your hands until it feels soft. Do not rupture the lemon.
5. Push the pieces of paper clip and wire into the lemon so that they are as close as possible without touching.
6. Moisten your tongue with saliva, and touch the tip of your wet tongue to the free ends of the paper clip and wire pieces.

Results A slight tingle may be felt and a metallic taste is detected.

Why? A **battery** is a device that uses chemicals to produce current electricity (energy due to the movement of electrons). The lemon battery you have created is called a voltaic battery. A **voltaic battery** is made up of two different metals called **electrodes** (where electric current enters or leaves the battery), which are placed in a liquid containing an **electrolyte** (a substance whose water solution can conduct electricity). In a solution of water plus an electrolyte (such as the acid in the lemon), an excess of electrons collects on one of the electrodes (copper wire), at the same time as electrons are lost from the other electrode (steel paper clip). Touching the electrodes to your tongue closes the **electric circuit** (the path through which an electric current flows) and allows an electric current to flow. The tingle felt and the metallic taste are due to the conduction of electricity through the saliva on your tongue.

steel paper clip
copper wire
lemon

201. Sliders

Purpose To determine which is the best heat conductor: metal, wood, or plastic.

Materials 3 spoons, wooden, plastic, metal
1-pint (500-ml) jar
margarine
3 plastic beads or dry beans of equal size
hot tap water

Procedure
1. Place the bowls of the spoons in the jar.
2. Use equal-size, but as small as possible, blobs of margarine to secure the plastic beads to the handles of the spoons. All the beads must be at the same height from the bottom of the jar.
3. Fill the jar about three-fourths full with hot water.
4. Observe the beads and note which one moves first.

Results Some of the margarine on the metal spoon melts and the margarine and attached bead slide down the spoon. The beads on the plastic and wooden spoons do not move.

Why? Hotter molecules in a material move more quickly and bump into colder molecules and transfer energy to them. Heat travels in all materials, but some materials are better conductors of heat than others. As a rule, solids conduct heat better than liquids, and liquids better than

gases. But some solids, such as metals, are very good conductors, while other solids, such as wood and plastic, are poor conductors, as seen in this experiment. This is because the wood and plastic have so many air spaces. Air is a good **insulator** (something that restricts or retards heat flow), so it is a poor conductor of heat. When hot water was poured into the jar, the spoons got warm. The metal spoon quickly conducted more of the heat, so the margarine on the metal spoon was heated, melted, and slid down the spoon, carrying the attached bead with it.

202. Restrictor

Purpose To determine whether sand has insulating properties.

Materials cardboard box at least 2 inches (5 cm) taller and wider than one of the jars
ruler
sand
two 1-quart (1-liter) jars with lids
1-cup (250-ml) measuring cup
hot tap water
2 bulb-type thermometers

Procedure
1. Cover the bottom of the box with 1 inch (2.5 cm) of sand.
2. Set one jar in the box and fill the box with sand up to the top of the jar.
3. Use the measuring cup to add 2 cups (500 ml) of hot water to each jar, then stand one thermometer in each jar of water for 1 minute.
4. Read and record the temperature of the water in each jar, then remove the thermometers and seal the jars.
5. Quickly cover the jar in the box with a 1-inch (2.5-cm) layer of sand. Close the lid on the box.
6. Allow the jars to remain undisturbed for 10 minutes.
7. Uncover the jars and stand one thermometer in each jar. Allow the thermometers to stand for 1 minute.

8. Read and record the temperature of the water in each jar.

Results The water in the jar that is placed in the box surrounded by sand stays warmer longer than the water in the uncovered jar.

Why? Heat energy moves from a warm area to a cooler area. As heat flows from the warm water to the materials outside the jars, the water in the jars cools. The water in the jar that is placed in the box surrounded by sand stays warmer longer because the heat is slowly conducted out of the water into the sand. The heat leaves the water in the uncovered jar more quickly as it flows to the cooler air outside. A good insulator, such as the sand, slows the energy flow.

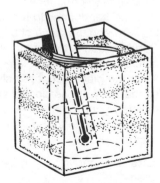

203. Trapped

Purpose   To compare the insulating properties of paper and Styrofoam cups.

Materials   2 ice cubes of equal size
two 10-ounce (300-ml) paper cups
two 10-ounce (300-ml) Styrofoam cups
timer

Procedure
1. Put an ice cube inside one of the paper cups.
2. Slip the second paper cup inside the first one so that it rests on top of the ice cube.
3. Repeat steps 1 and 2, using the 2 Styrofoam cups.
4. Lift the top cups and observe the ice cubes once every 5 minutes. Continue until one of the ice cubes completely melts.

Results   The ice cube in the paper cups melts first.

Why?   Styrofoam is a better insulator than paper. This is due to the amount of air trapped in the Styrofoam material. Air, like most gases, is a poor conductor of heat because the particles in a gas are far apart. Gas particles don't bump into each other very often, so gas doesn't transfer heat from one particle to the other very well. Since gases don't conduct heat well, they are good insulators. Thus, Styrofoam with its trapped air is a good insulator.

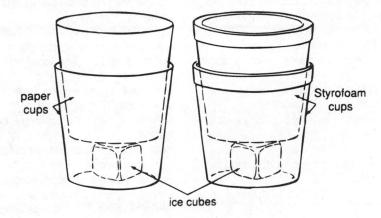

paper cups

Styrofoam cups

ice cubes

Glossary

abdomen   The hind part of an insect's body.

absorb   To take in.

absorption   The process by which one substance absorbs another, such as a dry bean or a sponge soaking up water.

acid   A type of chemical that produces hydrogen ions when dissolved in water and that turns blue litmus red.

action force   A force applied to an object.

adhesive force   The attraction between unlike molecules, such as water to paper.

agents of erosion   Wind, water, and ice.

altitude   The angular distance of a celestial body above the horizon.

amylase   A chemical in saliva that breaks down starch.

antioxidant   A substance that inhibits oxidation.

apparent magnitude   A measure of how bright a celestial body appears to be.

arc   Part of a circle.

arteries   Blood vessels that carry oxygen-rich blood from the heart throughout the body.

asterism   A group of stars that form a shape within a constellation.

asthenosphere   The portion of Earth's mantle that is below the lithosphere.

astrolabe   An instrument used to measure the altitude of celestial bodies.

astronomical unit (AU)   The distance from Earth to the Sun.

astronomy   The study of the planets, the stars, and other bodies in space.

atmosphere   The blanket of gases surrounding a celestial body.

atom   The smallest building block of matter, made up of a nucleus that has electrons spinning around it.

attraction   The force that draws things together.

autumnal equinox   A day of equal daytime and nighttime all around Earth, on or about September 23, when the Sun is directly overhead at the equator.

axis   An imaginary line that passes through the center of an object and around which the object rotates.

azimuth   The distance of an object, such as a star or any celestial body, in degrees clockwise around the horizon from due north.

ballooning   A technique that spiderlings use to float through the air and move to new areas.

base   A type of chemical that produces hydroxide ions and turns red litmus blue.

battery   A device that uses chemicals to produce an electric current.

biology   The study of the way living organisms behave and interact.

bolus   The food ball prepared in the mouth and swallowed.

bonds   Forces that link atoms, groups of atoms, or molecules together.

buoyant   Able to float in or on the surface of a fluid.

capillaries   Tiny blood vessels that connect the ends of arteries to the ends of veins.

carbonates   Chemicals containing combinations of carbon and oxygen with some other element, such as calcium, barium, or manganese.

carotene   A yellow or orange pigment in plants.

celestial   Heavenly.

celestial bodies   Natural objects in the sky, such as stars, suns, moons, and planets.

celestial pole   The location in the sky where Earth's axis points.

celestial sphere   An imaginary picture of the sky in which Earth is pictured at the center of a large, hollow sphere and all other celestial bodies are stuck on its inside surface.

cell   The smallest units or building blocks of all living things.

cell membrane   The thin, filmlike outer layer that holds a cell together and separates it from its environment, and allows materials to pass into and out of the cell.

cementation   A process of rock layer formation in which water is squeezed out, leaving minerals that glue the sediments together.

center of gravity   The point on an object at which its weight seems to be concentrated so that the object would balance if supported at this point.

centrifugal force   The force that causes a spinning object to tend to move outward from the center.

chemical change   A process by which one or more substances are changed into one or more different substances.

chemical indicator   A substance, such as litmus, that is used to determine the presence of an acid or a base.

chemical particles   The atoms or molecules that make up minerals and all matter.

chemical weathering   The breakdown of rocks by changes in their chemical composition.

chemistry   The study of the way materials are put together and their behavior under different conditions.

chlorophyll   A green plant pigment.

chloroplast   The part of a plant cell where chlorophyll is stored and food is made.

chlorosis   The loss of green color in plants.

chromatography   A method of separating a mixture into its parts.

circumference   The distance around a circle.

cleavage   The property of a mineral that allows it to break along a cleavage plane, exposing two smooth edges.

cleavage plane   A flat smooth area in minerals along which the bonds between atoms are relatively weak.

coagulate   To clump.

cohesive force   The attraction between like molecules, such as water to water.

coma The large gas and dust layer around the nucleus of a comet.

comet A small celestial body made up of interstellar dust and gases that revolves around the Sun.

compact Squeezed together.

compass rose A circle divided into 360° numbered clockwise from due north that is used to determine the azimuth of stars.

compound eyes The eyes of some insects, which are made up of thousands of ommatidia.

compressed Squeezed together.

compression The most dense part of a sound wave.

concentrated Gathered closely together.

condense To change from a gas to a liquid by cooling.

conduction The process by which some energy, including electricity, heat, and sound, travels through a material.

conifers Nonflowering plants that reproduce by forming cones.

constellation A group of stars that appear to make a pattern in the sky.

continuous spectrum A spectrum in which the colors are arranged in a continuous order of red, orange, yellow, green, blue, indigo, and violet.

contour lines Lines on a map connecting points on Earth that have the same elevation.

contraction Squeezing together.

cotyledons The two halves of a seed that are actually simple leaves; also called seed leaves.

crescent The moon phase in which there is a small lighted area resembling a segment of a ring with pointed ends.

crust The outer layer of Earth.

crystal A solid material in which the atoms or molecules are arranged in a repeating pattern.

cup The English unit for liquid volume.

current electricity Energy due to the movement of electrons.

cytoplasm A grayish jellylike material made mostly of water that fills a cell, and in which the other parts of the cell float.

dark-line spectrum A continuous spectrum crossed by dark lines.

dehydrate To lose water.

dehydrating Removing water from a substance such as food.

dense The measure of how compact a material is.

density A measure of how much material of an object is packed into a given volume, calculated by dividing the mass of an object by its volume.

diffuse To spread apart and move freely in all directions.

digest To change food into a form that can be absorbed by the body.

displaced Pushed out of place.

dissolving The process by which a solute thoroughly breaks up and mixes with a solvent to form a solution.

dust tail The tail of a comet that is made of dust that glows white because it reflects sunlight.

earthquake A sudden movement or shaking of Earth's crust.

Earth science The study of Earth.

earthshine The light reflected from Earth's surface onto the Moon.

Eastern Hemisphere The eastern half of Earth between longitudes 0° and 180°.

echo A sound that is heard when sound waves bounce back from a surface.

echolocation A method of finding the direction and distance of objects by the sounds reflected from them.

echo time The time it takes for a sound to go out and come back.

eclipse The passing of one body in front of another, cutting off its light.

eclipsing binary system A star pair in which both stars revolve around a common point, and as viewed from Earth, one star periodically eclipses the other.

ectothermic Having a body temperature that changes with the temperature of the environment.

effort arm The distance from the fulcrum to the point on a lever where the effort force is applied.

effort force The force applied to do work.

electrical conductors Materials that allow electric charges to pass through them.

electric current A flow of electricity.

electricity A form of energy that comes from electric charges.

electrodes The part of a battery where electric current enters or leaves.

electrolyte A substance whose water solution can conduct electricity.

electrons The negatively charged particles spinning around the nucleus of an atom.

elements Substances made up of chemically identical particles.

elevation Height above sea level.

embryo An organism in its earliest stags of development.

energy The ability to cause changes in matter.

epicotyl The part of a plant embryo located above the hypocotyl that develops into the plant's stem, leaves, flowers, and fruit.

equator The imaginary line that circles Earth midway between the North and South Poles at latitude 0°.

equatorial diameter Diameter at the equator.

eroded Worn away.

esophagus The strong muscular tube that leads from the back of the throat to the stomach.

evaporate To change from a liquid phase to a gas phase.

evergreen Having leaves that remain green all through the year.

facet A lens on the surface of the ommatidium of an insect's compound eye.

fatty acids Chemicals found in animal and plant fat that are composed of carbon, hydrogen, and oxygen.

first-class lever A lever in which the fulcrum is between the two ends of the bar.

first quarter The moon phase following the new moon, in which half of the side of the Moon facing Earth is lighted.

fluid A substance that can flow, such as a liquid or a gas.

force Causes a change in motion.

fossil fuels Energy sources, including coal and natural gas, made of buried remains of decayed plants and animals that lived hundreds of millions of years ago.

fracturing The breaking of a mineral across a cleavage plane, exposing uneven or jagged edges.

free-fall   To fall only to the pull of gravity.

friction   The resistance to motion of two materials moving against each other.

frost   A light deposit of ice crystals that forms when water vapor changes into a solid.

fulcrum   A fixed point that a lever pivots around.

full moon   The moon phase in which the side of the Moon facing Earth is fully lighted.

gas   The phase of matter characterized by no definite shape or volume—for example, air.

geocentric   Earth-centered.

germinate   Process by which a seed begins to grow.

gibbous   The moon phase in which more than half of the side of the Moon facing Earth is lighted.

global warming   An increase in the average temperature of Earth.

gores   Lone, pointed, elliptical sections.

gravity   The force of attraction between two bodies; the force that pulls objects toward the center of Earth.

great circle   A circle on a sphere in which the center of the circle and the center of the sphere are the same point.

half-life   The time it takes for half the atoms in a given sample of a radioactive element to decay.

hardness   (1) A measure of the amount of calcium, magnesium, and/or iron salts dissolved in water. (2) The resistance of a mineral to being scratched.

head   The front body part of an insect.

heart rate   The number of times your heart beats in 1 minute.

heliocentric   Sun-centered.

hilum   The scar on a seed coat where the seed was attached to its pod.

homogeneous   Being a solution that is the same throughout.

horizon   The imaginary line where the sky appears to meet Earth.

humidity   The amount of water in the air.

hurricane   A large tropical storm with winds of 74 miles per hour (118 kph) or more that rotate around a relatively calm center.

hydrated   Being in a state in which solute molecules are surrounded by water molecules, or in which materials, such as food cells, contain water.

hydration   Process by which water molecules surround a solute molecule.

hydrometer   An instrument used to measure the density of a liquid.

hydrophilic   Having an attraction for water.

hygrometer   An instrument used to indicate changes in humidity.

hygroscopic   Able to absorb water from the air.

hypocotyl   The part of a plant embryo that develops into the lower stem and root.

igneous rock   Rock produced by the cooling and solidifying of magma and lava.

imbibe   To absorb water.

imbibition   The process by which a hydrophilic, porous material absorbs water.

inclined plane   A simple machine made of a flat, slanting surface used to raise an object.

inertia   A property of matter that causes objects to resist any change in motion.

inferior planets   The planets Mercury and Venus, which are in orbit between Earth and the Sun.

inhibit   To decrease or stop an action.

insoluble   Unable to be dissolved.

insulator   A material that restricts or retards the flow of heat and is therefore a poor conductor of heat.

interstellar dust   Small particles of matter between celestial bodies.

ion   Charged particle.

ion tail   The tail of a comet that is composed of gas ionized by solar wind and glowing with a blue color.

ionized   Electrically charged.

kinetic energy   Energy of motion.

latitude   The distance in degrees north and south of the equator.

lava   Magma that has risen to the surface of Earth.

lens   The part of the eye that focuses light rays.

lever   A machine made of a rigid bar that pivots around a fulcrum and is used to lift or move a load.

lift   An upward force due to the flow of air over an object, such as the force which acts on the wings of an insect.

lines of latitude   See **parallels.**

lines of longitude   See **meridians.**

liquid   The phase of matter characterized by a definite volume but no definite shape—for example, water.

liter   The SI for liquid volume.

lithosphere   The layer of Earth made up of the crust and the upper portion of the mantle.

litmus   A substance obtained from lichen, a plantlike organism, that acts as a chemical indicator.

load   The object lifted or moved by a machine.

load arm   The distance from the load to the fulcrum of a lever.

longitude   The distance in degrees east and west of the prime meridian.

luminous   Giving off its own light.

lunar eclipse   An eclipse of the Moon that occurs when Earth comes between the Sun and the Moon so that Earth's shadow falls on the surface of the Moon.

machine   A device that makes work easier by changing the speed, direction, or amount of effort force applied.

magma   Liquid rock beneath Earth's surface.

magnetic field   The area of force around a magnet, in which the magnet affects the movement of metal objects.

magnetic north pole   A place near Earth's North Pole where the north magnetic pole of a compass needle points.

magnetic south pole   A place near Earth's South Pole where the south magnetic pole of a compass needle points.

mantle   The layer of Earth beneath the crust.

mass   The amount of matter in an object. Scales are designed to compare weight and mass using the conversion of 454 equals 1 pound.

matter   Any substance that has mass and takes up space.

megaphone   A device used to make a person's voice sound louder.

melting   The change of a solid to a liquid as a result of an increase in energy.

melting point   The temperature at which a solid melts.

meridians   Imaginary lines that circle Earth from North Pole to South Pole; half of a great circle passing through the poles.

mineral   A substance found in the ground that does not come from living things, and has a definite chemical composition and a regular crystal form.

mixture   A physical combination of two or more substances.

molecules   The smallest parts of a substance that have all the properties of the substance.

moon phases   The apparent changes in the Moon's shape due to the revolution of the Moon around Earth.

movable pulley   A pulley that multiplies the effort force by moving in the direction of the force.

nebula   A cloud of interstellar dust and gas spread across many millions of miles (kilometers) in space.

neutral   Chemicals that are neither an acid nor a base.

neutrons   The neutrally charged particles in the nucleus of an atom.

new moon   The moon phase in which the Moon is between Earth and the Sun. The side of the Moon facing the Sun is lighted, so the side facing Earth is dark.

Newton's third law of motion   The scientific principle that states that for every action there is an equal and opposite reaction.

night vision   The ability to see in the dark.

non-Newtonian fluid   A substance that has properties of both solids and liquids.

Northern Hemisphere   The region of Earth north of the equator.

North Pole   The northernmost point on Earth.

north pole   The end of a free-swinging magnet that points toward the magnetic north pole of Earth.

North Star   See **Polaris.**

nuclear change   A change in the nucleus of an atom in the process of transmutation, resulting in the release of energy and matter.

nucleus   (1) The central part of the head of a comet. (2) The control center that directs all the activities of a cell. (3) The positively charged center of an atom, which contains protons and neutrons.

odor   The property of a substance that activates the sense of smell.

ommatidium (plural **ommatidia**)   One unit of an insect's compound eye, at the surface of which is a facet.

opaque   Not allowing light to pass through.

optical double   Two stars that only appear to be very close together but are actually far apart and have no relationship to each other.

orbit   The curved path of one body around another.

overfishing   The act of removing fish from the water faster than they can reproduce and be replaced.

ovipositor   An egg-laying tube in female insects.

oxidation   The process by which a substance is oxidized.

oxidize   To combine with oxygen.

Pangaea   The name given to the large, single landmass believed to have existed during the age of the dinosaurs.

parallax   The apparent shift in position of an object when viewed from different places.

parallels   Imaginary lines that circle Earth from east to west; also called lines of latitude.

partial solar eclipse   An eclipse in which part of the light of the Sun is blocked by the Moon.

penumbra   The lighter part of a shadow.

peristalsis   Muscle contractions inside the body to move substances, such as food, along.

perpendicular   At a right angle.

phases of matter   The three common forms of matter: solid, liquid, and gas.

phloem tubes   The tubes in a plant that transport sap containing water and food manufactured in the leaves throughout the plant and down to the root where it is stored.

physical change   A change in the appearance of matter, but not in its properties and makeup.

physical combination   A combination in which the parts retain their separate properties and can be separated.

physics   The study of energy and matter and their relationship.

phytoplankton   Small, often microscopic, plantlike water-dwelling organisms that are capable of using light to produce food.

pigment   A substance that colors and can protect an organism from ultraviolet light; used by plants to make food.

pitch   How high or low a sound is. Faster vibrations produce a higher pitch.

pivot point   The place on an object about which the object rotates; fulcrum; center of gravity.

planet   One of the nine celestial bodies that orbit the Sun; from a Greek word meaning wanderer.

plasticity   The ability of a solid material to flow.

plumule   The tiny immature leaves at the end of the epicotyl, which develop into the plant's first true leaves.

pod   A plant casing that holds seeds of some plants, such as peas and beans.

polar ice   The large masses of ice in the arctic and antarctic regions.

Polaris   The star near the north celestial pole toward which Earth's axis generally points; also called the North Star or Pole Star.

Pole Star   See **Polaris.**

pollen cone   The small cone of an evergreen that contains pollen and forms in groups at the tip of a branch.

porous   Having many tiny holes that allow fluids to pass through.

precession   The circular movement of Earth's axis.

predator   An animal that kills other animals for food.

pressure   The amount of force on an area.

prime meridian   The internationally accepted meridian that runs through Greenwich, England, at 0° longitude and is the starting point for measuring longitude.

proboscis   The coiled feeding tube of moths, butterflies, and some other insects.

protons   The positively charged particles in the nucleus of an atom.

pulley   A simple machine consisting of a grooved wheel that turns by the action of a rope or belt in the groove.

radiation   Energy in the form of rays or waves; energy given off when radioactive elements decay.

radicle   The tip of a hypocotyl, which develops into roots.

radioactive   Giving off radiation.

radioactive decay   The breakdown of the unstable nucleus of an atom.

radioactive element   Elements whose atoms undergo radioactive decay.

rarefaction   The least dense part of a sound wave.

reaction force   A force equal to an action force, but in the opposite direction.

reconstitution   The process of rehydrating dried food.

refractive telescope   A telescope with two main lenses, an objective lens and an eyepiece, which is used to study the stars.

regolith   The loose, uncemented rock particles, including soil, that cover the Earth.

rehydrating   Changing a dehydrated material to a hydrated form by restoring water to the material.

repulsion   The force that keeps things separate or apart.

retrograde motion   The apparent backward or westward motion of a planet in relation to the stars.

revolve   To move around a center point.

rotate   To turn on an axis.

rust   Iron oxide formed by the oxidation of iron in the presence of water.

rusting   The process by which a substance rusts.

saliva   A liquid in the mouth that softens and breaks down food.

satellite   A body that orbits a celestial body, including natural satellites (such as moons orbiting planets) and manufactured satellites (such as weather satellites orbiting Earth).

second-class lever   A lever in which the load is between the fulcrum and the effort force applied.

sediment   Regolith that has been transported by agents of erosion and deposited in another place.

sedimentary rock   Rock formed by deposit of sediments.

seed coat   The protective outer covering of a seed.

seed cone   The larger cone of an evergreen that contains seeds and usually forms as a single cone away from the tip of a branch.

SI   International System of Units, commonly called the metric system of measurement.

slope   The degree of steepness of an inclined surface.

snow   Soft white ice crystals.

solar eclipse   An eclipse of the Sun that occurs when the Moon comes between the Sun and Earth, blocking the Sun's light, so that the Moon's shadow falls on the surface of Earth.

solar energy   Energy from the Sun.

solar noon   The moment when the Sun is at its highest altitude and casts the shortest shadows.

solar wind   An energetic stream of charged particles constantly moving away from the Sun.

solid   The phase of matter characterized by a definite shape and volume—for example, ice.

solute   A material that dissolves in a solvent.

solution   A combination of a solute and a solvent.

solvent   The material in which a solute dissolves.

sound   Vibrations traveling through air or other materials.

Southern Hemisphere   The region of Earth south of the equator.

South Pole   The southernmost point on Earth.

south pole   The end of a free-swinging magnet that points toward the magnetic south pole of Earth.

specific gravity (S.G.)   The ratio of the mass of a substance compared to the mass of an equal volume of water.

spectroscope   An instrument that separates visible light into a spectrum.

spectrum   A band of colored lights produced when visible light is separated.

spiderling   A young spider.

spinneret   A spider's silk-spinning organ, which produces threads of silk form the secretion of silk glands.

standard time   The local (clock) time in a time zone.

starch   A complex chemical found in many foods.

static charges   Electric charges that are stationary.

static electricity   Energy due to the buildup of charges on an object.

stethoscope   A medical instrument used to listen to sounds within the body, specifically those made by the heart and lungs.

stomach   The pouch where the bolus is further digested.

stratum (plural **strata**)   A layer of one kind of rock material.

streak   The color of the powder left when a mineral is rubbed against a rough surface that is harder than the mineral.

stress   A deforming force.

stridulation   The process by which some insects make sounds by rubbing body parts together.

sublimation   The process by which a gas changes directly into a solid without becoming a liquid.

summer solstice   The longest day of the year in the Northern Hemisphere, on or about June 21, and on or about December 22 in the Southern Hemisphere.

surface tension   The attractive force that causes the molecules of a liquid to cling together to form a skinlike film at the liquid's surface.

synchronous rotation   The motion in which an object rotates once during one revolution around another object, such as the Moon around Earth.

tabular   Shaped like a tabletop.

tension   A type of stress by which rocks are stretched or pulled apart.

third-class lever   A lever in which the distance of the effort force is multiplied so that the effort arm is always shorter than the load arm.

third quarter   The moon phase following the full moon, in which half of the side of the Moon facing Earth is lighted.

thorax   The middle body part of an insect, to which the legs and wings are attached.

time meridian   The north-south line in the center of each time zone with 7.5° of longitude on each side of the line.

time zones   The 24 internationally accepted divisions of Earth, each about 15° of longitude wide, represent the 24 hours of the day.

topographic map   A flat map that uses contour lines to show the shape and height of a land area.

torque   The measure of a turning effect; determined by multiplying a force times the length of its torque arm.

torque arm   The distance from a pivot point to the point on an object where a turning force is applied.

total solar eclipse   A solar eclipse in which all of the Sun's light is blocked because the Moon is close enough to Earth that the apparent size of the Moon and the Sun are the same.

transmit   To send from one place to another.

transmutation   The process by which the nucleus of an atom changes so that a new element is formed.

transparent   Allowing light to pass straight through.

Tropic of Cancer   Latitude 23.5°N.

Tropic of Capricorn   Latitude 23.5°S.

ultraviolet light (UVL)   Light from the Sun that in excess can be dangerous to humans or other life-forms.

umbra   The darker part of a shadow.

valves   Flaps of tissue that control the flow of blood or other liquids in the body.

vapor   Gas.

vaporize   To change to a vapor.

veins   Blood vessels that carry oxygen-poor blood back to the heart.

vernal   Spring.

vernal equinox   A day of equal daytime and nighttime all around Earth, on or about March 21, when the Sun is directly overhead at the equator.

vibration   A repeated back and forth motion.

viscometer   An instrument that measures a liquid's viscosity.

viscosity   A measure of how fast a fluid flows.

viscous   Thick.

volume   The amount of space something occupies.

voltaic battery   A battery made up of two electrodes in a solution containing an electrolyte.

waning   Growing smaller.

water cycle   The natural process by which water from oceans, lakes, soil, and other sources on Earth evaporates, condenses in the atmosphere to form clouds, falls back to Earth in forms such as rain or snow, and returns to the oceans, lakes, and soil.

water wave   A disturbance on the surface of water that repeats itself.

waxing   Growing larger.

weight   A measure of the gravitational force pulling an object downward toward Earth's center; also the gravitational force between two objects.

weightlessness   A state of having no weight.

Western Hemisphere   The western half of Earth between longitude 0° and 180°.

winter solstice   The shortest day of the year in the Northern Hemisphere, on or about December 22, and on or about June 21 in the Southern Hemisphere.

work   The use of a force to move an object.

xanthophyll   A pale yellow pigment in plants.

xylem tubes   The tubes in a plant that transport water and dissolved minerals upward through the roots to the rest of the plant.

Index